FRUIT
for all seasons

COMPILED BY JENNENE PLUMMER

PHOTOGRAPHY BY
QUENTIN BACON AND ASHLEY BARBER

TORMONT

ACKNOWLEDGEMENTS
The publishers would like to thank the following people and organizations
for their assistance during the production of this book:

Sue Dodd and the Sydney Market Authority for the following recipes:
Blueberry and Goat's Cheese Salad
Berry Flan
Ruby Clafoutis
Passionfruit Sauce
Banana Soufflé
and for the transparency reproduced on page 41

Yvonne Webb for the following recipes:
Fish Shashlik
Lemon Sherbet
Fruit-filled Dumplings

Sherringhams Nursery, North Ryde, for fruit trees

Designer: Leonie Bremer-Kamp
Design Assistant: Russell Jeffery
Food Editor: Jennene Plummer
Editorial Assistant: Suzanna Norton

This edition is published with the permission of
HarperCollins Publishers Pty Limited.

Published in 1994 by
Tormont Publications Inc.
338 Saint Antoine St. East
Montreal, Canada H2Y 1A3
Tel. (514) 954-1441
Fax (514) 954-1443

ISBN 2-89429-388-7

Cover photography by Studio Tormont.
Chapter opening photography by Quentin Bacon,
with stylist Jennene Plummer

Printed in Canada.

Contents

FRUIT FOR ALL SEASONS

For snacks, appetizers, main courses and great finishes, fruit is the answer. It's delicious, it's easy to prepare, it's full of vitamins and minerals and it's so good. A platter piled high with fresh fruits is undoubtedly one of the most simple and refreshing ways to end a meal.

NATURE'S BOUNTY

Since classic times, the symbol of abundance has been the cornucopia – a horn of plenty overflowing with ripened fruit. *Fruit for All Seasons* brings you an abundance of tantalizing recipes using nature's fabulous bounty.

FRUIT FOR HEALTH

With people becoming more and more health conscious, fruit is a definite asset in the fresh food revolution that is quietly changing our eating patterns.

FRUIT FOR VARIETY

Many people think that fruit belongs only in desserts, jams and punches – now they can think again. Fruit can add a tangy vibrancy and melt-in-the-mouth texture to all sorts of savory dishes.

The range of fruit available to us today seems limitless. From the exotic and unusual to the more familiar, fruit is an abundant source of great taste and good nutrition.

Whether it comes to us from trees, vines or bushes, fruit can be served with little or no preparation; however, with just a little imagination, you can transform it into a feast of culinary delights.

Within a meal, fruit is traditionally served as a dessert or a refreshing appetizer, but it need not be limited to these roles. Fruit sauces complement meat, poultry and even fish dishes beautifully. Fruit

combined with salad ingredients adds a special tang. Fruit and cheese is a simply delicious way to end a meal – whether casual or formal. And for an added touch, why not dip a few strawberries in a little melted chocolate!

And, let's not forget the delights of homemade jams and chutneys or fresh fruit shakes.

FRUIT BOWLS

Fruit's versatility extends beyond cooking. Scoop the contents out of fruits such as grapefruit, cantaloupe, large oranges, pineapple, watermelon and avocado to create fruit shell serving dishes.

FRUIT'S TENDER TOUCH

Fruit is also a natural tenderizer. Wrap papaya leaves around meat or octopus overnight or marinate meats in papaya

juice or the juice of kiwis – they are the ideal natural tenderizers.

FRUITFUL TIPS

This book is filled with hints and tips to help make preparing these simple recipes even easier (including how to choose and store the various fruits). There are also notes on the best time to buy in our Pick of the Crop chart at the end of the book.

FRUIT DELIGHTS

We know the recipes in our book will inspire you to create your own fresh and innovative combinations, or to experiment with the new, exotic, more unfamiliar fruits now available.

Whatever your choice, fruit will delight your eye and palate throughout the year – spring, summer, autumn and winter. It is truly fine fare for all seasons.

APPLES *and* PEARS

Apples are, without doubt, one of the most popular fruits. Thanks to cultivation over the years, there are now over 3,000 known varieties. Whether green, red or yellow, their fresh flavor and crisp texture are unmistakable and appetizing on just about any occasion.

Cooking apples are normally green and cook down well to a purée. Try apples in salads, pies, or tarts; or baked, fried as an accompaniment to meat (especially pork or game) or made into fritters. Look for apples with tight, smooth, unmarked skin. Avoid those with bruises or cuts.

Apples keep very well.

Pears come in many different shapes and sizes, and are equally delicious whether firm or juicy ripe. Pears ripen very quickly, so buy while still firm and allow them to ripen in a cool, dark place. Keep pears refrigerated if you want them to last longer. Pears are popular poached, wrapped in pastry, in salads, with cheese, and in soufflés, sherbets and jams.

Recipes in this section cover ideas from soups through to cakes and preserves. We have also included recipes using Asian pears as well as figs.

STEWING FRUIT

When stewing fruit, use minimal water. Berries, rhubarb and juicy fruits need only a few spoonfuls, while other fruit (such as apples) should be half covered. To maintain shape of fruit when stewing, always boil sugar and water together first before adding the fruit. Simmer gently until tender.

TO SAUTÉ

Sautéing is a quick cooking method meaning to toss food in a pan in a little fat over high heat.

CHILLED PEAR *and* LIME SOUP

1 cup (250 mL) white sugar

4 cups (1 L) water or pear nectar

4 pears peeled, cored and puréed

juice of 6 limes

1 cup (250 mL) white wine

3 tbsp (45 mL) grated lime zest

1¼ cups (310 mL) sour cream

1 Place sugar and water in an 8-cup (2 L) saucepan. Over low heat, stir until sugar is dissolved. Bring to a boil. Reduce heat and simmer for 5 minutes.

2 Add puréed pears, lime juice and white wine. Simmer for further 10 minutes.

3 Remove from heat. Set aside to cool. Stir in lime zest and sour cream. Transfer to soup tureen or bowl. Chill and serve.

SERVES 8

CURRIED CHICKEN SOUP

2 tbsp (30 mL) butter

1 large onion, peeled and chopped

2 celery stalks with green tops, chopped

¼ cup (60 mL) all-purpose flour

1 tbsp (15 mL) curry powder

2 large green apples, roughly chopped

½ lb (225 g) cooked chicken meat, chopped

5 cups (1.25 L) chicken stock

1 tbsp (15 mL) lemon juice

salt and pepper, to taste

GARNISH

plain yogurt or whipping cream

chopped fresh chives

1 Melt butter in a large pan. Sauté onion and celery for about 5 minutes until softened. Add flour and curry powder and continue cooking for 3 minutes, stirring occasionally to prevent sticking.

2 Stir in apple, chicken and 1 cup (250 mL) of stock. Simmer for about 5 minutes. Cool slightly.

3 Purée mixture in a food processor or blender. This may need to be done in several batches. Return purée to pan. Add the remaining chicken stock, lemon juice and seasonings.

4 Bring to a boil. Simmer for about 10 minutes, cool, cover and chill in refrigerator. Serve cold with a spoonful of yogurt or whipping cream in each bowl and a sprinkling of chopped chives.

SERVES 4

Curried Chicken Soup

RED CABBAGE *and* APPLE

2 tbsp (30 mL) butter

**1 medium-size red cabbage,
finely shredded**

3 tbsp (45 mL) honey

1 small onion, peeled and grated

1 apple, grated

1 pear, peeled and chopped

¼ cup (60 mL) red wine

3 tbsp (45 mL) lemon juice

1 Melt butter in a large pan and sauté the cabbage with the honey. Add the onion, apple, pear, wine and lemon juice. Bring to a boil.

2 Simmer, covered, for 1 hour, shaking pan occasionally during cooking.

SERVES 6–8

APPLE *and* DATE SALAD *with* CALIFORNIAN SALAD DRESSING

**3 crisp apples, cored and chopped
to make 4 cups (1 L)**

1 cup (250 mL) pitted, chopped fresh dates

½ cup (125 mL) slivered almonds

4 crisp lettuce leaves

CALIFORNIAN SALAD DRESSING

1 tbsp (15 mL) Worcestershire sauce

1 tbsp (15 mL) olive oil

1 tbsp (15 mL) lemon juice

grated rind of ½ lemon

1 Mix apples, dates and almonds together with dressing. Pile in lettuce leaf cups.

2 TO PREPARE CALIFORNIAN SALAD DRESSING: Combine ingredients together in screw-top jar and shake well.

SERVES 4

 **PREPARING APPLES**

When apples and pears are cut, they turn brown due to oxidation. To prevent this, toss them in lemon juice.

Always core apples before you peel them if you want them to stay whole. They tend to collapse if cored after peeling.

Apple and Date Salad with Californian Salad Dressing

Mulligatawny Soup

 MULLIGATAWNY SOUP

Serve with a bowl of hot boiled rice and chapatti or pita bread. This spicy soup can also be made from beef, mutton or fish.

MULLIGATAWNY SOUP

1½ lbs (675 g) chicken pieces

4 cups (1 L) chicken stock

1 onion, peeled and sliced

1 carrot, peeled and sliced

1 stalk celery, sliced

2 tbsp (30 mL) butter

2 onions, peeled and finely chopped

2 green apples, peeled, cored and sliced

3 tbsp (45 mL) all-purpose flour

1 tbsp (15 mL) curry powder

1 bay leaf

¼ tsp (1 mL) allspice

5 tbsp (75 mL) cream

1 Place chicken pieces in a heavy saucepan. Add stock, onion, carrot and celery. Cover. Simmer for 1 hour.

2 Remove chicken pieces. Discard skin and bones. Cut chicken meat into small pieces.

3 Strain stock. Chill for 4 hours then remove fat from surface.

4 Melt butter in a saucepan. Sauté onions and apples together for 3 minutes. Stir in flour and curry powder. Cook 1 minute.

5 Add stock, bay leaf and allspice. Cover and simmer 15 minutes. Stir in chicken and cream. Continue cooking for 5 minutes until chicken is hot.

SERVES 8

CORIANDER *and* PEAR SALAD

The flavor of coriander and pear is delightful. A few pecans or walnuts may be added to give this salad extra crunch.

4 ripe Asian pears

1 bunch watercress

½ lb (225 g) cherry tomatoes

½ cup (125 mL) chopped fresh coriander leaves

½ bunch green onions, slivered

2 tbsp (30 mL) chives, snipped

DRESSING

½ cup (125 mL) olive oil

3 to 4 tbsp (45 to 60 mL) lemon juice

2 tsp (10 mL) Dijon mustard

1 clove garlic, peeled and crushed with a pinch salt

freshly ground black pepper

1 Peel, halve and core pears. Slice lengthwise. Arrange in a salad bowl lined with watercress. On top, scatter tomatoes, coriander, green onions and chives.

2 TO PREPARE DRESSING: Place all ingredients in a small bowl. Whisk together until combined. Pour over salad. Lightly toss just before serving.

SERVES 4

LAMB CURRY

Serve this curry with boiled rice, garnished with red pepper or lemon.

3 lbs (1.5 kg) boned shoulder or leg of lamb, trimmed and cubed

½ cup (125 mL) all-purpose flour

salt and freshly ground black pepper to taste

6 tbsp (90 mL) butter

2 green apples, peeled, cored and sliced

2 onions, peeled and chopped

1 tomato, quartered

2 cloves garlic, crushed

2 to 3 tbsp (30 to 45 mL) curry powder

1¾ cups (440 mL) stock or water

3 tbsp (45 mL) sultanas or raisins

3 tbsp (45 mL) shredded coconut

1 tsp (5 mL) brown sugar

grated rind and juice of ½ lemon

1 tbsp (15 mL) flaked almonds

1 Toss meat in flour combined with salt and pepper. Shake off excess.

2 Melt butter in a large pan. Add meat. Brown well. Remove from pan and set aside.

3 Add apples, onions, tomato, garlic and curry powder to pan. Cook for 2 to 3 minutes. Pour off any excess fat.

4 Stir stock into pan with all remaining ingredients except almonds. Return meat to pan. Simmer, covered, for 2 hours or until meat is tender. Stir in almonds.

SERVES 6

APPLE TIPS

Apples look attractive if presented cored and cut into rings or quartered, cored and sliced.

Apple skins provide lovely color, so leave them on unless told otherwise in the recipe.

PEAR TIPS

Pear flesh is extremely delicate, so handle with care.

If whole pears are required, core by working an apple corer in from the base or use a small spoon.

QUAIL *with* WILD RICE *and* APPLE

9 quail (1½ quail per serving)

8 juniper berries marinated 2 to 3 hours in ¼ cup (60 mL) Madeira wine

1½ cups (375 mL) chicken stock

STUFFING

2 tbsp (30 mL) butter

2 green onions, finely chopped

livers and hearts of quail, diced

1½ cups (375 mL) wild rice, cooked

1 large red apple, cored and diced

3 tbsp (45 mL) cream

1 egg yolk

salt and pepper to taste

pinch lemon thyme

MIREPOIX

2 tbsp (30 mL) butter

2 green onions, chopped

1 small carrot, diced

1 small stalk celery, diced

TO REDUCE

Reduce means to boil or rapidly simmer a mixture until evaporation occurs and the mixture thickens.

MIREPOIX

A mirepoix is a mixture of sautéed mixed vegetables used in meat, fish and shellfish dishes to enhance flavor.

1 With quails on their backs and starting at the tail end, make an incision along breast. Carefully remove all small bones from breast and back sections, leaving the legs intact.

2 TO PREPARE STUFFING: Melt butter in a pan. Add green onions. Cook until softened. Add the livers and hearts of quail. Cook 5 minutes. Mix in the wild rice and diced apple. Stir in cream and egg yolk to bind all ingredients together. Season to taste.

3 TO PREPARE MIREPOIX: Melt butter. Sauté vegetables until tender. Spoon into the bottom of an ovenproof dish.

4 Spoon stuffing into cavity of quails. Stitch incision with cotton thread. Arrange quails over mirepoix in one layer. Bake at 400°F (200°C) for 15 to 20 minutes, basting frequently. Lift quails from dish and remove stitches. Keep warm.

5 TO PREPARE SAUCE: Discard vegetables, but pour pan juices into a small saucepan. Add juniper berry mixture and chicken stock. Bring sauce to a boil. Reduce until thickened. Season, strain and spoon the sauce over the quails before serving.

SERVES 6

PEAR PROSCIUTTO

½ lb (225 g) prosciutto, thinly sliced

4 pears, peeled and sliced

2 kiwis, peeled and sliced

1 mango, peeled, seeded and sliced

GARNISH

cottage cheese

1 Arrange slices of prosciutto and fruits alternately on a large serving platter or 4 individual plates. Serve with cottage cheese.

SERVES 4

Quail with Wild Rice and Apple

APPLE STRUDEL

10 sheets filo pastry

¼ lb (110 g) butter, melted

1 cup (250 mL) fresh breadcrumbs

4 apples, peeled, cored and chopped

⅔ cup (165 mL) raisins

½ cup (125 mL) chopped walnuts

1 tsp (5 mL) cinnamon or mixed spice

4 to 5 tbsp (60 to 75 mL) rum or grated rind and juice of 1 lemon

½ cup (125 mL) white sugar

3 tbsp (45 mL) milk

¼ cup (60 mL) icing sugar

1 Brush 5 sheets of filo pastry with melted butter, placing one on top of the other. Set aside, covered with a damp tea towel. Repeat with remaining pastry sheets.

2 Scatter breadcrumbs over second stack of pastry. Spread with combined apple, raisins, chopped walnuts and spices. Sprinkle with rum and sugar.

3 Place the other stack of pastry over the fruit. Roll strudel up. Place on greased baking sheet. Brush top with milk.

4 Bake at 400°F (200°C) for 30 minutes. Place on serving plate and dust with icing sugar. Cut into slices. Serve warm.

SERVES 8–10

Apple Strudel

APPLE SPICE CAKE

1 lb (450 g) Granny Smith apples, peeled, cored, and sliced

5 tbsp (75 mL) water

juice of ½ lemon

¾ cup (185 mL) butter

½ cup (125 mL) brown sugar

3½ cups (875 mL) whole-wheat flour

1 tsp (5 mL) baking soda

1 tsp (5 mL) ground cinnamon

½ tsp (2.5 mL) ground nutmeg

½ tsp (2.5 mL) ground mace

¼ tsp (1 mL) ground cloves

1 cup (250 mL) chopped walnuts

1 cup (250 mL) chopped dates

⅓ cup (85 mL) raisins

¼ cup (60 mL) milk

TOPPING

1 tbsp (15 mL) brown sugar

¼ cup (60 mL) chopped walnuts

½ tsp (2.5 mL) cinnamon

1 Cook apples over low heat in water and lemon juice until soft. Mash with wooden spoon. Leave to cool.

2 Cream butter and sugar until light and fluffy. Sift flour with baking soda and spices into creamed mixture. Stir in, along with walnuts, dates, raisins, apple and milk. Spoon into greased 5 x 13 inch (12 x 33 cm) loaf pan.

3 TO PREPARE TOPPING: Combine topping ingredients. Sprinkle over cake. Bake at 350°F (180°C) for 1¼ to 1½ hours. Leave to rest in pan for 15 minutes. Turn out onto a wire rack to cool.

 SIFTING FLOUR

When sifting whole-grain flours, tip any leftover grains into mixture, don't throw them away.

Pear Tart with
Frangipani Cream

blind at 400°F (200°C) for 10 minutes. Cool before filling.

2 Cook pears in water, sugar and lemon rind until just tender. Cool in syrup. Drain on paper towel.

3 TO PREPARE FRANGIPANI CREAM:
Cream butter and sugar together. Add eggs a little at a time, beating well. Combine almonds, flour and kirsch. Beat into creamed mixture.

4 Spoon half the Frangipani Cream over pastry base. Arrange pear halves on this, cut-side facing down. Spread the remaining cream mixture around and over the pears.

5 Bake at 350°F (180°C) for 40 minutes or until cream is set and golden-brown on top. Brush with apricot jam.

SERVES 8

PEAR TART *with* FRANGIPANI CREAM

2 sheets ready-made shortcrust pastry

4 pears, peeled, halved and cored

2 cups (500 mL) water

1 cup (250 mL) sugar

strip of lemon rind

¾ cup (185 mL) apricot jam, warmed and sieved

FRANGIPANI CREAM

¼ lb (110 g) unsalted butter

½ cup (125 mL) sugar

2 large eggs, beaten

1 cup (250 mL) ground almonds

1 tbsp (15 mL) all-purpose flour

a few drops of kirsch or almond extract

TO BAKE BLIND

Line pastry with aluminum foil and dried beans or uncooked rice. Bake at 400°F (200°C) for 5 minutes. Remove foil and beans. Bake a further 5 minutes. Allow to cool.

1 Line base and sides of a 10 inch (25 cm) quiche pan with pastry. Trim edges. Bake

APPLE *and* PLUM CRUMBLE

1 lb (450 g) cooking apples, peeled, cored and sliced

1 lb (450 g) plums, halved and pitted

1 cup (250 mL) white sugar

4-5 tbsp (60 to 75 mL) orange juice

¼ lb (110 g) butter, cubed

2¼ cups (560 mL) all-purpose flour, sifted

½ cup (125 mL) flaked almonds

grated rind of 1 orange

1 Place half the fruit in a large ovenproof dish. Sprinkle with ¼ cup (60 mL) sugar and the orange juice before placing remaining fruit in dish.

2 Work butter into flour until mixture resembles fine breadcrumbs. Stir in remaining sugar, almonds and orange rind.

3 Spread crumble mixture thickly over fruit. Bake at 350°F (180°C) for 35 to 40 minutes or until top is slightly golden. Serve immediately, with whipped cream or custard.

SERVES 6–8

STEP-BY-STEP TECHNIQUES

BAKED PEAR SURPRISE

Leave stems on peeled pears for a very attractive effect. This recipe can be used with other fruits such as apples and peaches. Or you can serve a variety of fruits prepared this way.

¼ lb (110 g) butter

4 to 5 tbsp (60 to 75 mL) sugar

4 to 5 tbsp (60 to 75 mL) ground almonds

pinch cinnamon

1 egg, separated

1 tbsp (15 mL) orange liqueur

4 eating pears, ripe and tender

1 lb (450 g) ready-made puff pastry

3 tbsp (45 mL) apricot jam

1 Make a stiff paste by creaming butter, sugar, ground almonds and cinnamon together. Gradually add egg yolk. Stir in orange liqueur.

2 Peel and core pears. Split in half. Fill centers with paste. Press the two halves together.

3 Roll out puff pastry into 4 oblong pieces, 4 x 8 inches (10 cm x 20 cm). Place a pear in the middle of each. Brush edges with water. Fold oblong to enclose each pear, retaining the pear shape. Make two small cuts at the top to allow steam to escape. Brush with lightly whisked egg white. Let stand for 15 minutes.

4 Place on greased baking sheet. Bake at 400°F (200°C) for 20 minutes.

5 Heat apricot jam until liquid. Strain. When pears are taken from oven, brush them lightly with hot jam as a glaze. Serve hot with ice cream or custard.

SERVES 4

Cream butter, sugar, cinnamon and almonds

Peel and core pears, split in half and fill centers

Enclose pear in pastry, retaining pear shape

APPLE ALMOND FLAN

PASTRY

1½ cups (375 mL) all-purpose flour

6 tbsp (90 mL) butter or margarine, cubed

1 egg yolk

1 to 3 tbsp (15 to 45 mL) lemon juice or water

FILLING

¼ lb (110 g) butter or margarine

½ cup (125 mL) white sugar

2 eggs

½ cup (125 mL) ground almonds

1 tbsp (15 mL) all-purpose flour

3 green apples, peeled, cored and thinly sliced

3 tbsp (45 mL) strained apricot jam (optional)

icing sugar for dusting

1 TO PREPARE PASTRY: Sift flour into a bowl. Cut in butter or margarine until the mixture resembles breadcrumbs.

2 Mix in egg yolk, and enough lemon juice to make a soft, pliable dough. Wrap in plastic wrap and let rest in refrigerator for at least 20 minutes.

3 TO PREPARE FILLING: Cream butter and sugar together until light and creamy. Beat in eggs, almonds and flour and set aside.

4 Roll out pastry to fit a greased 9 inch (22 cm) quiche pan. Trim edges. Refrigerate for 10 to 15 minutes.

5 Spread almond filling over pastry base. Smooth top.

6 Arrange apple slices decoratively over the filling, pressing in lightly.

7 Bake preheated oven at 375°F (190°C) for 15 minutes. Reduce temperature to 350°F (180°C) and bake for a further 25 to 30 minutes or until set and golden.

8 Heat jam gently. Brush over apples. Cool and serve dusted with icing sugar.

SERVES 8–10

Apple Almond Flan

FRESH FIG *and* APPLE JAM

1 lb (450 g) fresh figs, washed and sliced

2 cooking apples (about ½ lb or 225 g), peeled, cored and sliced

juice of 3 lemons

grated rind of 1 lemon

2 cups (500 mL) white sugar

1 Place figs and apples in large heavy saucepan with lemon juice and lemon rind. Cover and cook gently over low heat.

2 When fruit is very soft, add sugar. Stir until dissolved. Bring to a boil. Boil rapidly until setting point is reached or until temperature on candy thermometer is 210°F (105°C).

3 Spoon jam into hot clean jars, cover with waxed paper discs and seal.

MAKES ABOUT 2 LBS (1 KG)

APPLE BUTTER

1⅔ lbs (750 g) cooking apples

2½ cups (625 mL) cider

white sugar as needed

½ tsp (2.5 mL) ground cinnamon

½ tsp (2.5 mL) ground cloves

grated rind of ½ lemon

1 Wash, quarter and core apples, but do not remove skins. Place in large pan with cider. Bring to a boil. Simmer gently until apples turn pulpy.

2 Pass apples and cider through a sieve. Discard residue. Measure quantity of fruit purée and add 1½ cups (375 mL) white sugar for each 2½ cups (625 mL) purée. Return purée and sugar to pan.

3 Add spices and lemon rind. Stir purée over low heat until sugar dissolves. Stir constantly until mixture is very thick, creamy and almost solid.

4 Place in heated, sterilized jars. Seal and cool.

MAKES ABOUT 3 LBS (1.5 KG)

APPLE *and* PEAR MUSTARD

1 cup (250 mL) dry white wine

½ cup (125 mL) white grape juice

2 sticks cinnamon

pared rind of 1 lemon

¾ lb (340 g) green cooking apples, peeled, cored and diced

¾ lb (340 g) pears, peeled, cored and diced

⅓ lb (150 g) seedless green grapes, peeled

¾ cup (185 mL) Dijon mustard

½ tsp (2.5 mL) dark mustard seeds

1 Place wine, grape juice, cinnamon sticks and lemon rind in a saucepan. Bring to a boil. Simmer for 5 minutes.

2 Discard lemon rind. Simmer for a further 5 minutes. Discard cinnamon sticks.

3 Add fruit. Simmer for 15 to 20 minutes or until just tender. Carefully blend in mustard and seeds. Simmer for a further 2 to 3 minutes. Pour into warm, sterilized jars. Seal.

MAKES 3½ CUPS (875 ML)

 SETTING JAM

The setting point for jams and marmalades is best measured on a candy thermometer. If you don't have a candy thermometer, to test if set, place a little marmalade or jam on a cool plate. If the skin that forms wrinkles when pushed with a finger, the marmalade is set.

CITRUS

Oranges, lemons, limes, grapefruit, mandarins, tangerines and kumquats all belong to the citrus family. They span a spectrum of flavors from sharp and bitter to sweet and tangy, each enhancing cookery in very special ways.

Choose firm, bright, glossy, unblemished fruit with no soft spots. Store in a cool place. As the skin of mandarins is loose, they do not keep as well as tight-skinned oranges. If fruit has been cut, cover with plastic wrap, store in the refrigerator and use within a few days. Citrus fruit will keep in the refrigerator for several weeks.

Lemons and limes are traditional accompaniments to fish and seafood but also make wonderful desserts. Oranges are often included in salads and are used in many different desserts.

Our recipes cover ideas from soups, dressings and main dishes to candies and preserves. Their usage in cooking is almost endless.

Carrot *and* Orange Soup

1½ lbs (675 g) carrots, peeled and sliced

1 onion, peeled and chopped

2 stalks celery, chopped

4 cups (1 L) chicken or vegetable stock

1 bay leaf

1 tbsp (15 mL) cornstarch

grated rind and juice of 1 orange

good pinch nutmeg

seasoning to taste

4 to 5 tbsp (60 to 75 mL) cream (optional)

1 Place vegetables in a pan with the stock and bay leaf. Cover and simmer for 20 minutes, until the vegetables are tender. Purée vegetables in food processor or push through a sieve.

2 Blend cornstarch with a little of the soup.

3 Return the puréed vegetables to the soup with the blended cornstarch, orange rind and juice, nutmeg and seasonings. Bring to a boil. Simmer for 3 minutes, stirring.

4 Pour soup into a serving bowl. Decorate with a swirl of cream.

SERVES 6

Tabbouleh

Chop parsley and mint in a food processor for added convenience.

¾ cup (185 mL) bulgur (cracked wheat)

1½ bunches flat-leaf parsley, finely chopped

½ bunch green onions, finely chopped

½ cup (125 mL) finely chopped fresh mint

juice of 1 large lemon

4 to 5 tbsp (60 to 75 mL) olive oil

2 tomatoes, roughly chopped

salt and freshly ground black pepper

1 Soak bulgur in water to cover for 10 minutes or until all water is absorbed.

2 Place bulgur in a salad bowl with parsley, green onions and mint. Pour over lemon juice and oil. Lightly toss with tomato and seasonings.

SERVES 4–6

Citrus *and* Mango Salad *with* Cream Dressing

1 head of lettuce, leaves washed and dried

3 stalks celery, cut into 3 inch (8 cm) pieces

16 oz (450 g) can mango slices, drained

3 oranges, peeled and segmented

1 cucumber, scored and thinly sliced

6 green onions, thinly sliced

CREAM DRESSING

5 tbsp (75 mL) mayonnaise

½ cup (125 mL) cream

salt and freshly ground black pepper

3 tbsp (45 mL) chopped parsley

1 tsp (5 mL) Dijon mustard

1 tbsp (15 mL) orange juice

2 tsp (10 mL) lemon juice

1 Arrange lettuce leaves on a serving plate.

2 Make celery curls by slicing the celery lengthwise leaving one end uncut. Drop celery into ice water until it curls.

3 Arrange mango slices, orange segments, celery curls and cucumber on lettuce leaves. Garnish with green onions. Refrigerate until ready to serve.

4 TO MAKE DRESSING: Combine all ingredients. Let stand for 15 to 20 minutes before using. Serve separately.

SERVES 6–8

FRUITED CHICKEN SALAD

1½ to 2 cups (375 to 500 mL) cooked, diced chicken meat

½ cup (125 mL) brown long grain rice, cooked

2 grapefruit, peeled and segmented

2 carrots, cut into julienne strips

2 slices onion, separated in rings

1 large ripe avocado

3 tbsp (45 mL) lemon juice

1 tbsp (15 mL) vinegar

1 tbsp (15 mL) oil

lettuce leaves for serving

watercress, to garnish

DRESSING

½ cup (125 mL) mayonnaise

1 tsp (5 mL) curry powder

1 Place chicken, rice, grapefruit, carrots and onion into a salad bowl and toss well.

2 Peel and dice avocado. Brush with lemon juice.

3 Combine vinegar and oil. Add to chicken mixture with avocado and lemon juice and toss gently.

5 Serve salad on bed of lettuce. Garnish with watercress.

6 TO MAKE DRESSING: Combine all ingredients. Serve dressing separately.

SERVES 4

Fruited Chicken Salad

Arrange salad ingredients, marinate avocado

Combine oil and vinegar and add to salad

Blend salad dressing ingredients together

BROCCOLI SALAD *with* LIME MAYONNAISE

This tangy salad is served sprinkled with Italian Dressing and accompanied by Lime Mayonnaise.

3 large heads broccoli, cut into florets

ITALIAN DRESSING

3 tbsp (45 mL) wine vinegar

½ clove garlic, peeled and crushed

salt and freshly ground black pepper

1 cup (250 mL) olive oil

1 tbsp (15 mL) finely chopped fresh parsley

LIME MAYONNAISE

2 cups (500 mL) mayonnaise

2 cups (500 mL) light sour cream

⅓ cup (85 mL) freshly squeezed lime juice

1 tbsp (15 mL) finely grated lime peel

3 tbsp (45 mL) grated horseradish root

1 tbsp (15 mL) Dijon mustard

1 Place florets in a steamer. Steam over boiling water until just tender (approximately 3 minutes). If you have only a small steamer this can be done in batches.

2 When cooked, plunge instantly into ice water, taking care not to break the florets. Cool. Cover with plastic wrap. Refrigerate overnight.

3 TO PREPARE ITALIAN DRESSING: Combine vinegar, garlic, salt and pepper. Gradually whisk in oil and parsley. Sprinkle over broccoli florets just before serving.

4 TO PREPARE LIME MAYONNAISE: Whisk ingredients together in a bowl. This dressing can be prepared in advance and stored in the refrigerator. Serve separately.

SERVES 8–10

Florida Salad with Walnut Mayonnaise

 CITRUS SEGMENTS

To segment citrus fruit, peel all the skin and the white pith away. Cut down between the membranes with a very sharp knife and remove segments.

FLORIDA SALAD *with* WALNUT MAYONNAISE

3 tomatoes, diced

2 apples, diced

2 oranges, peeled and segmented

1 grapefruit, peeled and segmented

¼ cup (60 mL) mayonnaise

1 tbsp (15 mL) sugar

1 tbsp (15 mL) cream cheese

1 tbsp (15 mL) chopped walnuts

lettuce leaves to serve

1 Combine tomatoes, apples, oranges and grapefruit in a bowl.

2 Blend or process mayonnaise, sugar, cream cheese and walnuts together. Pour over the salad ingredients. Toss well. Cover and chill thoroughly before serving.

3 Serve on a bed of lettuce. Mayonnaise may be served separately.

SERVES 4–6

LEMON YOGURT DRESSING

An oil-free dressing made with fresh herbs that is ideal for papaya, grapes, melons and strawberries.

⅔ cup (165 mL) yogurt

1 tbsp (15 mL) finely chopped parsley

1 tbsp (15 mL) finely chopped chives

1 tbsp (15 mL) finely chopped thyme or mint

finely grated rind and juice of ½ lemon

freshly ground black pepper

1 Combine all ingredients in a screw-top jar. Shake to mix well. Refrigerate until required.

MAKES ⅔ CUP (165 ML)

AIOLI

This delicious garlic mayonnaise goes particularly well with fresh seafood.

12 to 16 cloves garlic, peeled and coarsely chopped

3 egg yolks

salt and freshly ground black pepper

2 cups (500 mL) olive oil

juice of 2 lemons

1 Purée garlic and egg yolks in a food processor or blender. Add salt and pepper.

2 With motor still running, add oil in a thin stream, slowly at first. As the sauce thickens, add lemon juice.

3 Taste, adding a little more lemon juice, salt or pepper if necessary.

MAKES 2½ CUPS (625 ML)

LEMON GRASS CHICKEN

Before using the shrimp paste, wrap the amount required in a small piece of aluminum foil and roast in a dry frying pan for a few minutes. Cool and use as required.

4 stalks lemon grass, thinly sliced

½ bunch green onions, chopped

1 onion, peeled and chopped

1 tsp (5 mL) shrimp paste

1½ cups (375 mL) coconut milk

1 tbsp (15 mL) demerara sugar

1 tbsp (15 mL) curry powder

2 lbs (1 kg) chicken pieces, skin removed

juice of 1 lemon

5 tbsp (75 mL) oil

3 tbsp (45 mL) sambal oelek
(chopped Thai chili pepper)

½ cup (125 mL) water

2 lime leaves or ½ tsp (2.5 mL) lime peel

salt and freshly ground black pepper,
to taste

1 Place lemon grass, green onions, onion, shrimp paste and ½ cup (125 mL) coconut milk in a food processor. Process to make a fine paste.

2 Mix sugar and curry powder together in a small bowl. Rub chicken pieces with lemon juice. Spread curry mixture over chicken. Allow to marinate for about 1 hour.

3 Heat oil in a heavy ovenproof casserole. Add sambal oelek. Cook, stirring, for 1 minute.

4 Add chicken. Fry until golden brown. Add lemon grass mixture, the remaining coconut milk, water, lime leaves and seasonings. Simmer uncovered for 35 minutes or until chicken is tender and sauce thickens slightly. Serve with steamed rice.

SERVES 4–6

 ZEST

The outer layer of citrus fruit skin is known as zest. It may be removed by using a grater (ensure only the color of the skin is removed, as the white pith underneath is bitter) or may be peeled off using a vegetable peeler. These pieces of skin may be sliced thinly, blanched and used in recipes. A zester will make even finer strips, and this peel does not require blanching.

 LEMONS AS GARNISH

Lemons make wonderful garnishes for many dishes, sliced, twisted, cut into wedges and so on.

OSSO BUCO ALLA MILANESE

8 pieces veal shank

all-purpose flour

6 tbsp (90 mL) butter or margarine

1 small onion, peeled and thinly sliced

1 small carrot, scrubbed and sliced

1 small piece celery, sliced

1 clove garlic, peeled and sliced

salt and freshly ground black pepper

½ cup (125 mL) white wine

2 cups (500 mL) canned tomatoes

1 cup (250 mL) beef stock

GREMOLATA

5 tbsp (75 mL) chopped fresh parsley

1 clove garlic, peeled and finely chopped

grated zest of 1 lemon

1 Dust veal in flour. Melt butter in a pan and brown the veal well.

2 Add the onion, carrot, celery, garlic and seasonings. Stir and turn veal occasionally.

3 When everything in the pan has acquired a lovely golden color, add wine. Simmer until liquid has almost completely evaporated.

4 Add the sieved tomatoes and stock. Cook slowly for just over an hour or until the meat is so tender it falls easily from the bone. If the sauce becomes too thick, add a few spoonfuls of water.

5 TO PREPARE GREMOLATA: Combine parsley, garlic and grated lemon. Serve osso buco sprinkled with gremolata.

SERVES 4

Fish Shashlik

FISH SHASHLIK

Bamboo skewers should be thoroughly soaked in water to prevent burning during cooking.

4 to 5 tbsp (60 to 75 mL) lemon juice

4 to 5 tbsp (60 to 75 mL) sour cream

2 lbs (1 kg) large firm-fleshed fish cut in 2 inch (5 cm) chunks

bamboo skewers, soaked in water

1 Combine lemon juice and sour cream. Dip each piece of fish in the sauce, then thread onto skewers.

2 Cook shashliks under a broiler for 5 to 6 minutes, turning constantly. Baste fish during cooking with any leftover lemon mixture. When ready, the fish will be golden. Serve with salad.

SERVES 4–6

POACHED OYSTERS *with* WATERCRESS SAUCE

24 oysters, in the shell

1 to 2 lemons

1 bunch watercress

cream

1 bouquet garni

1 tbsp (15 mL) finely chopped onion

1 tbsp (15 mL) finely chopped carrot

½ cup (125 mL) dry white wine

1 cup (250 mL) water

1 Remove oysters from shell and place in a bowl with their liquid.

2 Carefully peel rind off lemons, making sure no pith is included. Cut lemon rind into julienne strips and blanch in boiling water for 3 minutes. Drain, refresh in cold running water and set aside.

3 Pick leaves from watercress. Wash leaves well then blanch in boiling water for 4 minutes. Drain well and purée in a blender or food processor. Measure out ⅔ cup (165 mL) of purée and dilute with sufficient cream so that it will lightly coat an oyster. Keep warm.

4 Place remaining ingredients in a pan and simmer for 5 minutes.

5 Remove vegetables and bouquet garni. Add oysters to pan and poach over gentle heat for 2 minutes. Drain and put oysters back in shells.

6 Divide oysters between 4 serving plates and coat with watercress sauce. Garnish with lemon strips.

SERVES 4

LEMON JUICE

To extract the maximum amount of juice from a lemon, cook in the microwave on HIGH (100%) power for 20 seconds; or ensure they are at room temperature and roll on the counter for a few minutes before squeezing.

Poached Oysters with Watercress Sauce

Cut lemon rind into julienne strips

Place remaining ingredients in a pan and simmer for 5 minutes

Drain poached oysters and replace in shells

TO GRATE A COCONUT

Pierce the coconut through the 'eyes' and pour out liquid. Break the coconut open with a hammer by tapping around the middle. Pry out the meat with a knife. Remove skin with a vegetable peeler. Grate in a food processor. This may be frozen.

BROILED CRAYFISH

2 large green crayfish tails

salt and cayenne pepper

juice of 1 lemon

4 to 5 tbsp (60 to 75 mL) olive oil

fresh lemon thyme and rosemary leaves

watercress to garnish

1 Cut crayfish tails in half lengthwise. Season flesh of crayfish with salt and cayenne pepper, then brush with lemon juice and olive oil. Sprinkle with a few leaves of the herbs.

2 Place on a broiler pan and cook under a preheated broiler for 15 to 20 minutes, basting occasionally with a little olive oil.

3 When crayfish are lightly browned, arrange on a serving plate and garnish with watercress. Serve with green salad and crusty bread.

SERVES 4

LIME RICE

juice of 4 to 5 limes

½ cup (125 mL) coconut flesh, grated

1 tsp (5 mL) turmeric

½ tsp (2.5 mL) salt

2 cups (500 mL) rice, cooked

¾ cup (185 mL) clarified butter (see Note)

½ cup (125 mL) mustard seeds

1 cup (250 mL) chopped cashews

6 green chili peppers, seeded and chopped

2 curry leaves, chopped

1 tbsp (15 mL) finely chopped coriander leaves

GARNISH

1 lime, sliced

1 Add lime juice, coconut, turmeric and salt to cooked rice. Set aside.

2 Heat clarified butter. Fry mustard seeds until they pop. Add cashews, chili peppers and curry leaves. Cook for 3 minutes, stirring. Combine with rice and coriander leaves. Mix well.

3 Cook, covered, over low heat for 15 minutes to heat through. Garnish with lime slices.

NOTE: To clarify butter, melt it gently, skim off foam and discard sediment.

SERVES 6

Lime Rice

Mix lime juice, coconut, turmeric and salt with cooked rice

Combine cashew nuts with curry leaves and green chili peppers

Mix chopped coriander leaves with rice and cook slowly for 15 minutes

ROSE GERANIUM SHERBET

A cool dessert that is ideal served with spicy meals.

1½ cups (375 mL) granulated sugar

2½ cups (625 mL) water

grated rind and juice of 6 lemons

4 rose geranium leaves, lightly crumpled

1 egg white

rose geranium flowers and extra leaves for decoration

1 Place sugar in a medium-size saucepan with water and lemon rind. Stir over low heat. When sugar has dissolved, bring to a boil.

2 Add crumpled leaves. Boil for 6 minutes. Let cool.

3 Add lemon juice to cooled syrup. Pour mixture into cold freezer trays or a metal bowl. Place in freezer until mixture just begins to freeze.

4 Remove and turn into a bowl. Discard geranium leaves. Beat with a whisk until smooth, but not melted.

5 Beat egg white until stiff but not dry. Fold lightly through mixture. Return to tray. Cover. Freeze until firm.

6 Spoon sherbet into chilled glasses. Serve decorated with a rose geranium flower and leaves.

SERVES 2–4

Rose Geranium Sherbet

CANDIED PEEL

Prepare candied peel in your microwave oven by placing thin strips of peel from 2 oranges or lemons (or 1 of each) in a microwave-safe bowl with ½ cup (125 mL) white sugar and ½ cup (125 mL) water. Cook on HIGH (100%) power for 3 minutes, stirring once. Cook for 2 more minutes or until liquid is syrupy. Drain off syrup. Toss peel in some extra white sugar. When cool, store in an airtight container.

ORANGE SHERBET

A light, cool dessert for waistline watchers. If you own an ice cream maker, follow the manufacturer's instructions to freeze this recipe.

10 oranges
1 tbsp (15 mL) gelatine
3 tbsp (45 mL) water
½ cup (125 mL) extra water
sugar substitute, to taste
4 egg whites

1 Squeeze juice from oranges and strain.
2 Sprinkle gelatine over 3 tbsp (45 mL) water. Leave for a few minutes. Place container of gelatine in hot water. Stir until dissolved. Combine with orange juice and extra water. Blend in sweetener to taste.
3 Pour mixture into a cake pan. Freeze until half-frozen. Tip mixture into a bowl.
4 Beat well to break down ice crystals. Place in refrigerator.
5 Whisk egg whites until stiff. Fold into orange juice mixture. Return mixture to freezer in cake pan. Freeze until half frozen.
6 Turn into a bowl again and beat to break down ice crystals. Refreeze in pan. Beat once more if desired.

SERVES 10–12

 SPUN SUGAR

Prepare spun sugar in your microwave oven to make a very attractive garnish for many fruit dishes by dissolving ¼ cup (60 mL) white sugar in ¼ cup (60 mL) boiling water in a microwave-safe bowl. Cook on HIGH (100%) power for 3 to 4 minutes or until syrup is golden. Coat the back of 2 wooden spoons with toffee. Touch and draw spoons apart to form fine toffee strands. If toffee becomes too hard to work, cook on HIGH (100%) power in 20 second bursts until softened.

CHILLED LEMON SOUFFLÉ

1½ cups (375 mL can) evaporated skimmed milk
3 tbsp (45 mL) gelatine
5 tbsp (75 mL) water
grated rind and juice of 4 lemons
powdered or liquid sweetener, to taste
4 kiwis, peeled and sliced

1 Chill evaporated milk in refrigerator overnight.
2 Sprinkle gelatine over water. Let stand for a few minutes. Place container of gelatine in hot water. Stir until dissolved.
3 In a large chilled bowl, whisk milk until frothy. Beat in gelatine, lemon rind, juice and sweetener. The dessert should taste lemony – add more juice and rind if necessary.
4 Pour into a serving bowl. Refrigerate until set. To serve, arrange kiwis decoratively on top of soufflé.

SERVES 10–12

LEMON SHERBET

4 lemons
2 cups (500 mL) sugar
5 cups (1.25 L) water

1 Peel lemons, and remove pith and seeds. Finely chop pulp. Mix with sugar in a saucepan. Allow to stand for 2 hours.
2 Blend in water. Heat slowly, stirring constantly until sugar dissolves.
3 Pour into freezer trays or other suitable containers and freeze for 1 hour.
4 Remove from freezer. Beat vigorously for 2 minutes. Pour back into trays and freeze.

SERVES 6–8

Chilled Lemon Soufflé, Creamy Berries (page 40), Orange Sherbet

GRAPEFRUIT

Remove flesh easily from a grapefruit by halving and using a grapefruit knife to separate the flesh from the skin. Use a knife to cut between the segments. The flesh will scoop out easily with a spoon.

GLACÉ GRAPEFRUIT

1 orange
2 large grapefruit, halved
½ cup (125 mL) white sugar
4 to 5 tbsp (60 to 75 mL) medium sherry

GARNISH
extra orange and grapefruit segments
shredded peel
mint leaves
4 strawberries

1 Finely grate orange rind. Remove flesh from grapefruit, reserving skin. Peel and segment orange. Dice orange and grapefruit flesh.
2 Blend flesh with sugar, sherry and orange rind. Fill grapefruit halves with mixture. Freeze until set. Garnish with extra orange and grapefruit segments, shredded peel, mint leaves and halved strawberries.

SERVES 4

LEMON TART

1 quantity Orange Crust Pastry (see recipe following)
6 eggs
⅔ cup (165 mL) sugar
juice of 4 lemons
1½ cups (375 mL) whipping cream
¼ lb (110 g) butter or margarine, melted
extra cream
1 lemon, sliced, to garnish

1 Roll out pastry on lightly floured board to line a 10 inch (25 cm) quiche pan. Cover pastry with cooking parchment or foil and dried beans or uncooked rice (this is call baking blind). Bake at 400°F (200°C) for 5 minutes. Remove foil and beans. Bake further 5 minutes. Allow to cool.
2 Beat eggs and sugar until light and lemon colored. Stir in lemon juice, cream and butter. Pour into pastry shell.
3 Bake at 325°F (160°C) for 45 minutes or until firm. Spread with extra whipped cream. Garnish with slices of lemon.

SERVES 6

Glacé Grapefruit

ORANGE CRUST PASTRY

1¼ cups (310 mL) all-purpose flour, sifted
¼ cup (60 mL) unsalted butter, cubed
¼ cup (60 mL) margarine
1 tsp (5 mL) grated orange rind
3 tbsp (45 mL) orange juice

1 Place flour in a bowl. Cut in butter and margarine until mixture resembles bread-crumbs. Stir in orange rind.
2 Mix orange juice into flour mixture to form a soft dough. Wrap in plastic wrap. Refrigerate for 1 hour before rolling out.

STEP-BY-STEP TECHNIQUES

LEMON CURD

Orange curd can be made in the same way as lemon curd, using 4 small or 3 large oranges, preferably not too sweet.

4 lemons

¾ cup (185 mL) butter or margarine

2 cups (500 mL) sugar

4 eggs

1 Finely grate rind of 3 lemons. Cut lemons in half. Extract juice and discard pits.

2 Melt butter and sugar in double boiler or a bowl set over a pan of hot water. Stir until smooth, without boiling. Blend lemon rind and juice into mixture.

3 Beat eggs in another bowl. Whisk them into lemon mixture. Place over low heat. Continue to whisk, without boiling, until mixture is thick and creamy.

4 Meanwhile, heat clean jars in a low oven. When curd is ready, pour into jars. Cover curd surface with waxed paper discs.

5 Cover jars and leave to cool – the curd will set to a soft jammy texture. Store in a cool place and eat within a month.

MAKES APPROXIMATELY 2 LBS (1 KG)

BOTTLING HINTS

When bottling, use clean jars with no cracks or chips.

Seal jars when bottling with sterilized tight-fitting lids (boil them for 5 minutes) or tightly tie wax paper around neck of jar using elastic bands.

Lemon Curd

Melt butter and sugar in a bowl set over a pan of hot water. Stir until smooth

Blend the finely grated lemon rind and the juice into mixture

Beat the eggs and pour into the lemon mixture, stirring constantly. Continue to stir over low heat for 30 to 40 minutes until mixture is thick and creamy

Lemon Coconut Bars

LEMON COCONUT BARS

BASE

½ cup (125 mL) butter or margarine,
at room temperature

¼ cup (60 mL) sugar

½ tsp (2.5 mL) vanilla extract

1 cup (250 mL) self-rising flour

½ cup (125 mL) shredded coconut

TOPPING

¼ cup (60 mL) butter or margarine,
at room temperature

¼ cup (60 mL) condensed milk

juice and grated rind of 1 lemon

1 cup (250 mL) icing sugar

1 cup (250 mL) shredded coconut

1 TO PREPARE BASE: Cream butter and
sugar together. Blend in remaining
ingredients until well combined.

2 Press into a jelly roll pan. Bake at 350°F
(180°C) for 20 minutes. While cooking,
prepare topping.

3 TO PREPARE TOPPING: Combine all
ingredients for topping. Spread over base
while hot. Allow to set. Cut into fingers.

MAKES APPROXIMATELY 36 FINGERS

CITRUS RING COOKIES

1 cup (250 mL) all-purpose flour

¼ tsp (1 mL) allspice

⅓ lb (150 g) butter or margarine

½ cup (125 mL) white sugar

1 egg

grated rind of 1 lemon

1 cup (250 mL) ground almonds

2 cups (500 mL) fresh breadcrumbs

1 egg yolk, beaten

ICING

2 cups (500 mL) icing sugar, sifted

3 tbsp (45 mL) lemon juice

5 tbsp (75 mL) candied orange and
lemon peel

1 Sift flour and spice together. Cream butter
and sugar together until light and fluffy.
Beat in egg and lemon rind.

2 Fold in flour, ground almonds and breadcrumbs to make dough. Wrap dough in
plastic wrap. Chill for 1 hour.

3 Divide dough into 30 pieces and roll
each piece until 4 inches (10 cm) long.
Brush ends with egg yolk. Join together
to form ring. Place on greased baking pans.
Bake at 400°F (200°C) for 10 to 15
minutes. Cool on a wire rack.

4 TO PREPARE ICING: Blend together
icing sugar and lemon juice. Ice cookies.
Decorate with strips of candied peel.

MAKES 30

MIXED FRUIT CUP

1 papaya, peeled and seeded

2 bananas, sliced

4 cups (1 L) water

1 cup (250 mL) sugar

1 cup (250 mL) fresh orange juice

½ cup (125 mL) fresh lemon juice

pulp of 12 passionfruit

2 x 24 fl oz (2 x 750 mL) bottles soda water

ice cubes

10 strawberries, sliced

1 orange, thinly sliced

mint sprigs

1 Purée papaya and bananas in food processor or blender.

2 Boil water and sugar, stirring for 8 to 10 minutes until sugar dissolves and thin syrup is formed. Immediately pour into orange and lemon juices. Add puréed fruit and passionfruit. Chill until needed.

3 To serve, add soda water and ice cubes and garnish with strawberries, orange slices and mint leaves.

MAKES 12 CUPS (3 L)

GRAPEFRUIT MARMALADE

Prepare jars by placing in a large pot of boiling water. Simmer for a few minutes. Remove from water with tongs. Place upside down on baking pans. Allow to dry completely in a warm oven.

3 grapefruit, thinly sliced

12 cups (3 L) water

12 cups (3 L) sugar

1 tsp (5 mL) cream of tartar

1 Cover grapefruit with water. Allow to stand at least 12 hours. Cook, covered, over low heat until tender. Leave until the next day.

2 Bring slowly to a boil. Stir in sugar and cream of tartar. Stir until sugar dissolves.

3 Boil rapidly until marmalade gels when tested on a cool saucer. Bottle while hot in warm, sterilized jars. Seal when cold.

MAKES APPROXIMATELY 9 LBS (4 KG)

MARMALADE

Marmalade, that favorite breakfast preserve, is made from citrus fruits, using a method similar to but longer than jam-making. As with jam, the pectin found in the pith and pits of citrus fruit is the essential setting substance. The setting point is best measured on a candy thermometer. To test if set, place a little marmalade on a cool plate. If the skin that forms wrinkles when pushed with a finger, the marmalade is set.

Mixed Fruit Cup

Pour syrup into orange and lemon juices

Add puréed fruit

Stir in passionfruit and chill thoroughly

BERRIES

Berries are always associated with the summer months and come in a great variety. The most common, the strawberry, is soft, succulent and seductive. It is available all year round and is used to make many wonderful desserts. Its flavor, as with other berries, varies according to size and ripeness.

Other berries include blackberries, gooseberries, blueberries, mulberries, red and black currants, raspberries and loganberries. Should you desperately want to make something with any of these fruits and they are unavailable, the frozen or canned varieties work well, especially for sauces or purées.

When choosing strawberries, look for evenly colored, plump fruit with fresh green tops. Avoid baskets containing squashed fruit. Strawberries are highly perishable and should be used on the day of purchase, but will keep for a day or two, covered, in the refrigerator. Should any begin to mold, remove immediately as mold spreads quickly.

When choosing other types of berries, look for shiny, plump fruit in baskets without fruit stains.

Raspberries and blueberries can be frozen loose and uncovered on cookie sheets, and then packed in rigid containers. Blueberries also keep for up to 3 weeks in the refrigerator.

STRAWBERRY

*Always wash
strawberries before
hulling. If the stalks are
removed before washing,
water may be absorbed
into the fruit and ruin
the flavor.*

 BLUEBERRY

*Blueberries are used in
muffins, pancakes, pies,
cakes and cookies, in
sauces and stewed either
alone or with apples, pears
and quince. They go very
well with spices such as
cinnamon, coriander,
ginger, nutmeg and
cardamom. Serve fresh
with sour cream or cottage
cheese and brown sugar.*

BLUEBERRY *and* GOAT'S CHEESE SALAD

1 small loaf French bread

3 tbsp (45 mL) butter

16 slices goat's cheese,
½ inch (1 cm) thick

1 head red lettuce, washed

1 romaine lettuce, washed

2 Valencia oranges, segmented

1 grapefruit, segmented

⅓ lb (150 g) snow peas, blanched

½ cup (125 mL) blueberries

3 tbsp (45 mL) walnut oil

2 tsp (10 mL) white vinegar

1 tsp (5 mL) Dijon mustard

1 Slice French bread into 16 slices ½ inch
(1 cm) thick. Spread each slice with a little
butter. Place a slice of cheese on each. Place
on a baking sheet. Bake at 400°F (200°C)
until golden. Allow to cool.

2 Tear lettuce into bite-size pieces. Arrange
lettuce, citrus segments, snow peas and
blueberries on serving plates. Garnish with
toasted goat's cheese croutons.

3 Combine walnut oil, vinegar and
mustard. Sprinkle over salad.

SERVES 8

SUMMER SALAD *with* RASPBERRY VINAIGRETTE

1 head loose leaf lettuce, washed and dried

1 butter lettuce, washed and dried

1 small Spanish onion, thinly sliced

1 barbecued chicken, skin removed and cut
into bite-size pieces

1 mango, peeled and sliced

1 papaya, peeled and sliced

½ cup (125 mL) blueberries

½ cup (125 mL) halved pecans, toasted

**RASPBERRY
VINAIGRETTE**

½ cup (125 mL) olive oil

¼ cup (60 mL) raspberries

1 tbsp (15 mL) white wine vinegar

2 tsp (10 mL) honey

1 tsp (5 mL) sesame oil

¼ tsp (1 mL) Tabasco sauce

salt and freshly ground black pepper
to taste

1 Arrange all ingredients for salad in a
serving bowl. Toss well. Cover. Refrigerate
until required.

2 TO PREPARE RASPBERRY VINAIGRETTE:
Place all ingredients in a food processor or
blender. Process until smooth. Pour over
salad just before serving. Toss well.

SERVES 4–6

 BLACKBERRY

*Blackberries are very nourishing, containing a high
proportion of calcium and vitamin B1. They can be served
fresh or in jams or pies, etc. Because of their 'seedy' texture,
a lot of blackberry cooking requires straining the pulp and
using the extracted juice.*

 RASPBERRY

*Raspberries are one of the sweetest and most delectable of
berries. Raspberries can be eaten fresh, or served in
compotes, cakes, pies, tarts, flans, pancakes, jams or jellies.
Raspberries puréed with cream are a tasty dressing for
fruit desserts.*

STEP-BY-STEP TECHNIQUES

ICED SUMMER SALAD

½ basket strawberries, hulled

1 peach, peeled and seeded

1 banana, peeled

2 tsp (10 mL) sugar

8 oz (225 g) cream cheese

3 tbsp (45 mL) lemon juice

½ tsp (2.5 mL) ground ginger

3 tbsp (45 mL) whipping cream, whipped

¼ cup (60 mL) chopped hazelnuts

shredded lettuce

prepared vinaigrette dressing

1 Dice fruit. Sprinkle with sugar.

2 Beat cream cheese with lemon juice and ginger.

3 Fold in cream, fruit and nuts.

4 Pour mixture into 4 individual molds. Freeze for 1 to 2 hours or until firm.

5 Dip each mold into warm water. Turn salad onto a bed of shredded lettuce, if desired. Serve immediately with vinaigrette dressing.

SERVES 4

Sprinkle diced fruit with sugar

Fold in cream, nuts and fruit

Spoon mixture into individual molds

Iced Summer Salad

Fruit-filled Dumplings

3 Transfer dough to a floured board. Knead until dough is very smooth. Add extra flour if necessary.

4 Roll out until thin. Cut into small rounds about 2 inches (5 cm) in diameter.

5 **TO PREPARE FILLING:** Place fruit in a pan with sugar. Bring to a boil, stirring constantly. Take care that it does not burn.

6 **TO COMPLETE:** Place about 1 tsp (5 mL) of prepared filling on each round. Fold over. Pinch edges to seal. Pull out ends to form horns and curl under the base of dumpling.

7 Place on floured board with tails underneath until ready to cook.

8 Half fill a large saucepan with water. Bring to a boil. Drop in about 10 dumplings at a time. Simmer for 5 to 10 minutes, or until they rise to the surface.

9 Use a large perforated spoon to remove when cooked. Drain. Serve with extra fruit filling and cream.

COEUR *à la* CRÈME

1½ cups (375 mL) cottage cheese

8 oz (225 g) cream cheese

¼ cup (60 mL) whipping cream, whipped

1 tbsp (15 mL) icing sugar, sifted

icing sugar, extra

1 basket fresh raspberries, or 8 oz (225 g) frozen, thawed

1 basket fresh strawberries, to garnish

1 Cream together the 2 cheeses. Fold in cream and icing sugar.

2 Line 6 Coeur à la Crème molds with cheesecloth. Stand on a small tray. Spoon cheese mixture into molds. Smooth top. Refrigerate overnight.

3 Turn out molds onto 6 dessert plates. Remove cheescloth. Sift extra icing sugar over the top.

4 Purée raspberries in a food processor. Sweeten to taste with icing sugar if desired. Spoon sauce around each Coeur à la Crème. Garnish with strawberries.

SERVES 6

COEUR À LA CRÈME

Coeur à la Crème molds are white, heart-shaped molds available from cookware and department stores in the gourmet cookware section. Small ramekin molds may be used as a substitute.

FRUIT-FILLED DUMPLINGS

PASTRY

3 cups (750 mL) all-purpose flour, sifted

4 eggs yolks

2 cups (500 mL) warm milk

FILLING

1⅓ lbs (600 g) pitted cherries, strawberries, blueberries or pitted plums, washed

1 cup (250 mL) sugar, or as required

1 **TO PREPARE PASTRY:** Place flour in a large mixing bowl. Make a well in the center. Whisk together egg yolks and milk. Pour into well.

2 Slowly, with a wooden spoon, fold in flour until the dough forms a ball. Knead well. Cover with a cloth. Set aside for about 30 minutes.

Coeur à la Crème

HULLING STRAWBERRIES

Remove strawberry stalks (hulling) by twisting the leaves.

BERRY MUFFINS

3 cups (750 mL) all-purpose flour

1 tbsp (15 mL) baking powder

½ cup (125 mL) sugar

½ cup (125 mL) brown sugar

½ cup (125 mL) butter or margarine, melted

3 eggs

1 cup (250 mL) milk

1 to 1½ cups (250 to 375 mL) berries in season

icing sugar

1 Sift flour and baking powder into a bowl. Stir in sugars.

2 Combine butter, eggs and milk. Stir into dry ingredients until just blended.

3 Fold in berries very lightly. If large berries such as strawberries are used, cut into dice.

4 Spoon into greased muffin tins until two-thirds full. Bake at 400°F (200°C) for 15 to 20 minutes or until golden. Sprinkle with icing sugar while hot. Serve hot with butter.

NOTE: Do not worry if all the flour is not mixed in – 16 strokes is usually enough. This helps to give the characteristic texture of muffins.

MAKES 20-24

CREAMY BERRIES

3 baskets ripe strawberries

sugar, to taste

3 tbsp (45 mL) gelatine

5 tbsp (75 mL) water

6 egg whites

1 Purée berries with sugar. Sprinkle gelatine over water and let stand for 5 minutes. Place container of gelatine in hot water to dissolve, then stir gelatine into purée.

2 Whisk egg whites to form stiff peaks; fold into berries. Taste and adjust for sweetness. Spoon into serving bowl, cover and chill.

SERVES 10–12

MIXED BERRY PUDDING

8 slices white bread, crusts removed

3 tbsp (45 mL) brandy

6 cups (1.5 L) mixed berries, eg. strawberries, raspberries, blueberries, mulberries (see note)

½ cup (125 mL) sugar (see note)

3 tbsp (45 mL) water

cream to serve

1 Cut bread into fingers. Cover base and sides of a 4-cup (1 L) soufflé dish with bread, saving enough pieces to make a top.

2 Drizzle brandy over the bread on the base. Set aside.

3 Place fruit in a large pan with sugar and water. Cook over very low heat until the sugar has dissolved and the fruit is soft but not mushy (there should be plenty of juice).

4 Strain the fruit. Reserve juice. Drizzle 1 tbsp (15 mL) of juice over base of pudding. Spoon the fruit into the bread case.

5 Pour over all but ¼ cup (60 mL) juice. Top with remaining bread fingers. Pour over remaining juice.

6 Place a plate, small enough to fit inside the rim of the dish, on top of the pudding. Press down with heavy cans or weights. Refrigerate overnight.

7 Just before serving, remove the weights and plate. Invert onto serving dish. Serve with cream.

NOTE: If canned fruit is used, use juice and reduce sugar to ¼ cup (60 mL).

SERVES 4–6

BERRY PURÉES

Berry purées make delicious dressings. Add a little to your favorite vinaigrette for a refreshing change.

MAKING FOOD PROCESSOR PASTRY

When using a food processor to make pastry, be careful not to overmix as the pastry will be tough. It is best to use the 'pulse' to help prevent this.

BERRY FLAN

PASTRY

1½ cups (375 mL) all-purpose flour

3 tbsp (45 mL) white sugar

¼ lb (110 g) butter or margarine, cubed

1 egg yolk

1 tbsp (15 mL) ice water

FILLING

4 oz (225 g) cream cheese, softened

½ cup (125 mL) sour cream

½ cup (125 mL) icing sugar

1 tbsp (15 mL) brandy

TOPPING

1 basket raspberries

1 basket blueberries

extra icing sugar

1 TO PREPARE PASTRY: Place flour and sugar in food processor. Process until combined. Gradually add butter to the flour. Process until mixture resembles breadcrumbs.

2 Add egg yolk. Process until combined. With the motor running, add only enough water until pastry forms a soft ball.

3 Turn mixture out onto a lightly floured board. Knead lightly. Wrap in plastic wrap. Rest for 30 minutes. Roll out pastry to fit an 11 inch (28 cm) flan or quiche pan.

4 Blind bake at 400°F (200°C) for 10 minutes. Discard foil and rice, bake a further 5 minutes or until golden. Remove from oven. Let cool.

5 TO PREPARE FILLING: Place softened cream cheese and sour cream in food processor. Process until smooth. Add icing sugar and brandy. Combine well. Transfer to a bowl. Chill.

6 TO PREPARE TOPPING: Spoon filling into pastry shell. Arrange berries over the filling. Lightly dust with extra icing sugar. Chill.

SERVES 12

BLIND BAKING

Line pastry with kitchen parchment or foil and dried beans or uncooked rice. Bake at 400°F (200°C) for 5 minutes. Remove paper and beans. Bake further 5 minutes. Allow to cool.

Berry Flan

STONE FRUITS

With the summer comes the mouth-watering aroma and delectable flavor of stone fruits, which include all-time favorites like cherries, peaches, nectarines, apricots and plums. These fruits are perfect additions to all types of summer cooking, whether raw or cooked.

When purchasing cherries, look for shiny, plump, unblemished fruit, avoiding any that are split or soft. They will keep for several days in the refrigerator.

Peaches come in many varieties, but they all have either yellow or white flesh. If the flesh adheres to the pit, they are known as clingstone, and if it comes away cleanly they are known as freestone. They are delicious broiled, poached or used to decorate tarts. Look for firm fruit with yellow or white beneath the rose blush. They will keep refrigerated for about a week.

Plums also come in many varieties and are great puréed, poached, in jams, sherbets, ice creams or as a sauce to accompany pork, duck or goose. Choose undamaged fruit that is not too soft. The same applies to nectarines and apricots.

Cherry Soup

PORK ROAST *with* CHERRY SAUCE

6 to 9 lb (3 to 4 kg) pork loin

2 cups (500 mL) boiling water

3 tbsp (45 mL) oil

1 tbsp (15 mL) coarse salt

6 cloves garlic

12 small bay leaves

CHERRY SAUCE

½ cup (125 mL) pitted cherries

¼ cup (60 mL) corn syrup

3 tbsp (45 mL) vinegar

salt and freshly ground pepper, to taste

pinch nutmeg

pinch cinnamon

pinch ground cloves

1 Deeply score rind of pork into ½ inch (1 cm) diamonds. Place pork loin, skin side down, in a pan. Pour in boiling water. Bake at 400°F (200°C) for 15 minutes. Remove pan from oven. Drain off liquid, reserving it for basting.

2 Add oil to pan. Rub pork skin with salt. Insert cloves and bay leaves in score marks. Roast pork, skin side up, at 375°F (190°C) for 3 to 3½ hours. Baste with drained liquid every 30 minutes.

3 When cooked, remove from pan. Cover. Allow to stand for 20 minutes before carving.

4 TO PREPARE CHERRY SAUCE: Combine sauce ingredients in a saucepan. Bring to a boil. Simmer for 3 minutes or until heated through.

5 Carve pork. Serve sliced with Cherry Sauce.

SERVES 12

CHERRY SOUP

1 lb (450 g) ripe cherries, pitted

3 cups (750 mL) water

½ cup (125 mL) sugar

⅓ cup (85 mL) lemon juice

fresh mint or parsley for garnish

plain yogurt (optional)

 **TO PIT CHERRIES**

To pit cherries, push the pit through with a skewer or use a cherry stoner.

1 Bring cherries, water, sugar and lemon juice to a boil. Simmer gently for 10 minutes. Allow to cool.

2 Purée in a food processor. Chill thoroughly. 3 Serve garnished with mint or parsley and, if desired, 1 tsp (5 mL) of yogurt in each bowl.

NOTE: This recipe may also be served over crushed ice.

SERVES 6

BREAST *of* DUCKLING *with* APRICOT SAUCE

The stock and sauce can be prepared in advance.
The duck can be served warm or cool.

6½ lb (3 kg) duckling

1 bay leaf

few celery leaves

10 black peppercorns

few sprigs parsley

1 small onion, peeled and sliced

¼ cup (60 mL) white wine

mustard cress or watercress to garnish

APRICOT SAUCE

¾ cup (185 mL) dried apricots

salt and freshly ground pepper to taste

juice of ½ lemon

1 tbsp (15 mL) brandy

1 Dislocate the wing and leg joints of the duck. Cut off. Cut off the wing tips. Reserve. Keep the wings and legs for another recipe.

2 Cut the breast away from the backbone, leaving breast whole. Place the wing tips and backbone in a pan. Cover with water and bring to a boil. Spoon off any foam. Add bay leaf, celery leaves, peppercorns, parsley, onion and wine. Simmer, partially covered, for 1 to 1½ hours.

3 TO PREPARE APRICOT SAUCE: Strain the duck stock. Soak the apricots in 2 cups (500 mL) stock for 1 to 2 hours. Reserve remaining stock.

4 Cook the apricots in soaking liquid until tender. Purée in food processor. Add seasonings and lemon juice.

5 Stir in brandy. If the sauce is a little thick, thin it with reserved stock.

6 Prick the duck breast in several places with a skewer. Season lightly with salt. Place in a pan. Roast at 375°F (190°C) for 10 minutes. Reduce the heat to 350°F (180°C). Roast for another 20 minutes or until cooked as desired when tested.

7 Remove breast from oven. Let it cool to room temperature. Carefully peel off all the skin. Slice flesh neatly.

8 Pour ⅓ cup (85 mL) of sauce onto each of 4 plates. Arrange overlapping slices of duck and skin on top. Garnish with mustard cress or watercress. Serve any remaining sauce separately.

SERVES 4

CHICKEN *with* PLUM *and* LYCHEE SAUCE

3 lb (1.5 kg) chicken, cut in bite-size pieces

½ cup (125 mL) Chinese plum sauce

1 clove garlic, crushed

1 tbsp (15 mL) soy sauce

1 tsp (5 mL) minced fresh ginger

¼ tsp (1 mL) chili pepper sauce

1 tbsp (15 mL) oil

8 oz (225 g) can lychees, drained, reserving ¼ cup (60 mL) juice

¼ cup (60 mL) water chestnuts

¼ cup (60 mL) bamboo shoots, sliced

3 tbsp (45 mL) cornstarch

1 tsp (5 mL) sesame oil

1 Remove skin from chicken pieces. Marinate for 2 hours with plum sauce, garlic, soy, ginger and chili pepper sauce. Drain. Reserve liquid.

2 Add oil to wok. Heat. Stir-fry chicken pieces. Cover with lid. Simmer 5 minutes.

3 Add marinade juices. Cover. Cook a further 5 minutes. Add lychees, water chestnuts and bamboo shoots. Stir-fry 1 to 2 minutes.

4 Combine reserved lychee juice and cornstarch. Stir into wok. Bring to a boil. Simmer 3 minutes. Stir in sesame oil. Serve hot with steamed rice.

SERVES 6

TO MAKE A COULIS

Make a delicious coulis by placing ½ lb (225 g) of fruit of choice in a food processor or blender with 1 tbsp (15 mL) orange juice or liqueur of choice (eg. Grand Marnier, brandy, etc.). Process until smooth. Serve with sweet or savory dishes or just simply over ice cream.

WHEN FRESH IS UNAVAILABLE

Frozen or canned varieties of fruit may be substituted for fresh if fresh is unavailable.

TO STONE FRUIT

Pit stone fruit by running a knife around the middle. Twist apart. Remove pit.

STORING FRUIT

If storing fruit in the refrigerator, remove about 30 minutes before serving to ensure its full flavor is appreciated.

PLUM FLAN

PASTRY

1⅓ cups (335 mL) whole-wheat flour

6 tbsp (90 mL) butter, cubed

1 egg yolk

a little milk

FILLING

3 egg yolks

1¼ cups (310 mL) plain yogurt

¼ cup (60 mL) honey

½ tsp (2.5 mL) powdered cinnamon

1 lb (450 g) small plums, halved and pitted

½ cup (125 mL) blanched almonds

1 tbsp (15 mL) brown sugar

1 TO PREPARE PASTRY: Sift flour into a bowl. Cut in butter. Add egg yolk and enough milk to form firm dough.

2 Roll out to line an 8 inch (20 cm) flan or quiche pan. Prick base a few times with a fork.

3 TO PREPARE FILLING: Beat yolks with yogurt, honey and cinnamon. Pour into pastry shell.

4 Arrange plums, cut side down, in yogurt mixture. Bake at 400°F (200°C) for 35 to 40 minutes or until custard is set.

5 Sprinkle with nuts and brown sugar. Brown under a hot broiler.

SERVES 6

SUMMER FRUIT *with* SOUR CREAM

6 peaches, plums, apricots, nectarines or combination, peeled, halved and pitted

2 tsp (10 mL) white sugar

¼ cup (60 mL) Grand Marnier

1¼ cups (310 mL) sour cream

½ cup (125 mL) brown sugar

¼ cup (60 mL) flaked almonds, toasted

1 Place fruit cut side up in an ovenproof dish. Sprinkle with sugar.

2 Pour Grand Marnier over. Cover with plastic wrap. Refrigerate for several hours or overnight.

3 Remove from refrigerator 2 to 3 hours before serving. Just before serving, cover with sour cream. Sprinkle with brown sugar.

4 Place under a hot broiler until sugar caramelizes. Top with almonds. Serve immediately.

SERVES 6

RUBY CLAFOUTIS

1⅔ lbs (750 g) plums

½ cup (125 mL) all-purpose flour

½ cup (125 mL) sugar

4 eggs

1 cup (250 mL) milk

3 tbsp (45 mL) brandy

3 tbsp (45 mL) flaked almonds

extra sugar

1 Place plums in a large saucepan of boiling water. Simmer 2 to 3 minutes until just tender. Strain. Plunge into cold water to cool.

2 Halve plums. Remove stems and pits. Transfer to a lightly buttered ovenproof dish. Place flour and sugar in a bowl. Beat in eggs, one at a time. Add half the milk. Beat for 5 minutes. Stir in the remaining milk and brandy.

3 Pour mixture over the plums. Sprinkle with flaked almonds. Bake at 350°F (180°C) for 40 to 45 minutes. Sprinkle with extra sugar. Serve hot with cream.

NOTE: Apricots may be substituted for plums if desired.

SERVES 4

FRESH FRUIT SHORTCAKE

¼ lb (110 g) butter or margarine

¼ cup (60 mL) sugar

4 egg yolks

1½ cups (375 mL) all-purpose flour, sifted

TOPPING

2½ cups (625 mL) whipping cream, whipped

2 cups (500 mL) chopped fruit (peaches, nectarines, plums, apricots)

2 nectarines, halved, seeded and thinly sliced

1 Cream butter and sugar together until light and fluffy. Add egg yolks one at a time. Beat well after each addition. Mix in flour until well combined.

2 Knead dough on a lightly floured working surface. Place on greased pizza pan, using your knuckles or fingertips to press out to fit pan.

3 Bake blind (see page 14, Pear Tart with Frangipani Cream) at 350°F (180°C) for 20 to 25 minutes or until lightly browned. Remove from oven. When cold, gently lift shortcake onto serving dish.

4 TO PREPARE TOPPING: Combine cream and fruit. Spoon onto shortcake base. Arrange nectarine slices on cream with skin side showing. Serve slightly chilled.

SERVES 10–12

The shortcake base may be cooked up to 2 days ahead of time and stored in a covered container.

5 Spoon into individual chocolate cases. Chill for at least 2 hours before serving. Garnish with mint leaves.

SERVES 4

PEACH *and* PLUM FROZEN TERRINE

1 lb (450 g) peaches, peeled and pitted

½ cup (125 mL) orange juice

¼ cup (60 mL) white sugar

rind and juice of one lemon

1 lb (450 g) plums, peeled and pitted

½ cup (125 mL) orange juice, extra

¼ cup (60 mL) white sugar, extra

3 tbsp (45 mL) port

1 Place peaches, orange juice, sugar, and lemon rind and juice in a food processor or blender. Process until smooth. Pour into a jelly roll pan. Freeze.

2 Repeat with remaining ingredients. Freeze.

3 When both purées are icy but not solid, spoon half of the peach mixture into the base of a plastic-wrap-lined loaf pan. Smooth top.

4 Top with half the plum mixture. Smooth top. Repeat with remaining mixture to make 4 layers. Cover the surface with plastic wrap. Freeze overnight.

5 Remove the plastic from the top. Invert the terrine onto a serving plate. Remove remaining plastic.

6 Cut into ½ inch (1 cm) slices with a warm knife to serve. Garnish with slices of peaches and plums and a sprig of mint.

SERVES 8

Peach Chocolate Cups

PEACH CHOCOLATE CUPS

10 oz (300 g) dark chocolate, melted

6 peaches, peeled, seeded and roughly chopped

juice of 1 large lime

⅔ cup (165 mL) plain yogurt

1 tsp (5 mL) gelatine

2 tsp (10 mL) cold water

4 mint sprigs, to garnish

MELTING CHOCOLATE

Melt chocolate in your microwave in a microwave-safe bowl in short bursts on MEDIUM power (50%). Stir between each burst.

1 Lightly brush four 4 inch (10 cm) individual tart tins with oil. Spoon 3 tbsp (45 mL) melted chocolate into bottom of each. Using a pastry brush, spread chocolate evenly around the base and sides of tin.

2 Allow to set in refrigerator. Brush with extra chocolate if the cases are too thin. When solid, lift from tins carefully so as not to break edges.

3 Purée peaches, lime juice and yogurt in a food processor. Soften gelatine in cold water. Stir over a bowl of hot water until dissolved. Whisk into peach mixture.

FRUITY BRANDY SNAP BASKETS

Brandy Snap Baskets may be made several days in advance and stored in an airtight container.

BRANDY SNAP BASKETS

¼ cup (60 mL) butter or margarine

¼ cup (60 mL) brown sugar

¼ cup (60 mL) golden syrup or corn syrup

¼ cup (60 mL) all-purpose flour

½ tsp (2.5 mL) ground ginger

1 tsp (5 mL) lemon juice

¼ tsp (1 mL) vanilla extract

FILLING

1 tbsp (15 mL) rum (see note)

1 cup (250 mL) mascarpone (see note)

sliced pitted fruit of choice

1 TO PREPARE BRANDY SNAP BASKETS: Place butter, sugar and syrup in a small saucepan. Heat gently until butter has melted and sugar has dissolved. Cool.

2 Sift flour and ginger together. Stir into butter mixture with lemon juice and vanilla.

3 Place teaspoonfuls of the mixture onto greased cookie sheets. Allow room for spreading.

4 Bake at 350°F (180°C) for about 5 minutes or until golden. Allow to cool on pans for 1 minute.

5 Remove from cookie sheets with spatula. Place each over a greased upside-down glass. Shape into a basket with fingers. Continue with remaining mixture. Cool completely.

6 TO PREPARE FILLING: Blend rum into mascarpone. Spoon into baskets. Top with fruit just before serving.

NOTE: Other liqueurs may be used to flavor mascarpone. Mascarpone is an Italian-style cream cheese available from cheese shops.

MAKES ABOUT 12

BLACKFOREST CRÊPE CAKE

CRÊPE MIXTURE

2 cups (500 mL) all-purpose flour

2 ½ cups (625 mL) milk

2 eggs

2 tbsp (30 mL) butter or margarine

FILLING

16 oz (450 g) can pitted black cherries

¼ cup (60 mL) orange-flavored liqueur

3 tbsp (45 mL) sugar

3 tbsp (45 mL) cornstarch

1 cup (250 mL) whipping cream, whipped

¼ cup (60 mL) almond flakes, toasted

1 TO PREPARE CRÊPES: Sift flour into a bowl. Blend in milk and eggs to form a smooth batter.

2 Grease crêpe pan with butter. Pour ¼ cup (60 mL) crêpe mixture into hot pan. Turn pan to cover base thinly with mixture. Pour off excess. Cook for 1 to 2 minutes. Turn to cook other side.

3 Continue until 15 to 20 crêpes have been made. Layer crêpes between paper towels. Allow to cool.

4 TO PREPARE FILLING: Place cherries with their juice, liqueur, sugar and cornstarch in saucepan. Bring to a boil, stirring. Allow to thicken. Cool.

5 Spreading filling between each layer, forming crêpes into dome shape.

6 Coat outside of crêpes with whipped cream. Pipe crown of rosettes on top of cake. Decorate sides of cake with toasted almonds. Refrigerate until serving. Serve sliced.

7 To toast almonds, place in a dry frying pan. Toss over low heat until golden. Remove from pan. Cool.

SERVES 10–12

Peel peaches by dipping in boiling water for 30 seconds to 1 minute. Place immediately in cold water. The skin will come away easily. Apricots and plums are peeled in the same way.

CRÊPE BATTER

Crêpe batter should be the consistency of table cream. To achieve this, add more liquid as required.

PEACH MOUSSE

2 ripe peaches

1 tbsp (15 mL) lemon juice

almond or orange liqueur (optional)

1 cup (250 mL) whipping cream, chilled

2 egg whites

¼ cup (60 mL) sugar

Amaretti cookies, to garnish

1 Blanch peaches in boiling water for 30 seconds. Remove, plunge into cold water, then carefully peel. Slice peaches. Purée in food processor with lemon juice and liqueur.

2 Beat the cream until stiff. Chill. Beat egg whites until stiff peaks form, gradually adding the sugar until glossy.

3 Fold the whipped cream and meringue mixtures into the peach purée.

4 Spoon mousse into custard cups or glasses. Freeze 1 hour then transfer to refrigerator for 2 hours. Serve chilled but not hard, garnish with Amaretti.

SERVES 6

PEACH *and* DATE BARS

1½ cups (375 mL) whole-wheat flour

3 tsp (15 mL) baking powder

1 cup (250 mL) brown sugar

16 oz (450 g) can peach slices, drained and roughly chopped

½ cup (125 mL) dates, finely chopped

½ cup (125 mL) shredded coconut

½ cup (125 mL) hazelnuts, finely chopped

¾ cup (185 mL) butter or margarine, melted

1 Sift flour and baking powder into bowl. Add sugar, peaches, dates, coconut and hazelnuts. Mix in butter. Pour into a greased 9 x 13 inch (22 x 33 cm) pan.

2 Bake at 375°F (190°C) for 25 minutes. Allow to cool in pan, then cut into fingers. Store in an airtight container.

MAKES ABOUT 24

POACHED PEACHES

4 peaches

¼ cup (60 mL) shredded coconut

¼ cup (60 mL) ground almonds

1 egg yolk

½ tsp (2.5 mL) finely grated orange rind

2 tbsp (30 mL) butter or margarine

1 cup (250 mL) white wine

1 cinnamon stick

1 Plunge peaches into boiling water for 30 seconds. Drain. Cover with cold water. Peel, cut in half and remove pits.

2 Place peaches, cut side up, in an oven-proof dish. Combine coconut, almonds, egg yolk and orange rind. Spoon into peach cavities. Dot with butter.

3 Pour in wine and add cinnamon stick. Bake, covered, at 350°F (180°C) for 20 minutes or until peaches are tender. Remove cinnamon stick. Serve warm.

SERVES 4–8

HONEYED FRUITS

4 lbs (2 kg) stone fruits (plums, cherries, apricots and peaches)

3 tbsp (45 mL) honey

2⅓ cups (585 mL) rosé wine

1 Prepare fruit. Slice or halve according to size. Layer fruit in large glass serving dish.

2 Stir honey into wine. Pour over fruit. Leave overnight in refrigerator. Serve with yogurt or cream.

SERVES 12

PEACH ICE CREAM *with* FRESH PEACHES

3 large peaches
1½ cups (375 mL) whipping cream
1 tbsp (15 mL) Grand Marnier
½ cup (125 mL) sugar
¼ cup (60 mL) sugar syrup (see note)
1 tbsp (15 mL) chopped pistachio nuts

1 Pour boiling water over 1 peach in a bowl. Let stand 1 minute. Drain. Plunge into cold water, then remove skin and pit. Mash to make ½ cup (125 mL).

2 Combine peach pulp with cream, 2 tsp (10 mL) Grand Marnier and sugar in food processor. Blend until smooth and the sugar is dissolved. Pour into the container of an ice cream maker or into a freezer tray.

3 Churn or freeze until of ice cream consistency. If a freezer tray is used, beat lightly halfway through freezing. Place plastic wrap over trays to prevent ice crystals forming.

4 If an ice cream churn is used, remove ice cream from churn and store in a covered container in the freezer until required.

5 An hour before serving, peel the remaining peaches (as described previously) and cut each into 8 slices. Place in a bowl. Marinate with sugar syrup and the remaining Grand Marnier. Cover to prevent fruit discoloring.

6 Arrange the fruit slices in stem glasses. Place 2 scoops ice cream on top. Sprinkle with pistachio nuts. Serve with sponge finger cookies if desired.

NOTE: To make sugar syrup, boil for 2 to 3 minutes 1 part water to 2 parts sugar.

SERVES 4–6

Peach Ice Cream with Fresh Peaches

STEP-BY-STEP TECHNIQUES

PLUM JAM

4½ lbs (2 kg) plums

2½ cups (625 mL) water

9 cups (2 kg) sugar

1 Chop plums into sections and remove and reserve pits. Place fruit and water in a large saucepan. Simmer gently until plums are tender.

2 Meanwhile crack a few of the pits. Remove kernels and blanch them with boiling water to remove skins. Add kernels to fruit.

3 Remove pan from heat. Add sugar. Stir until completely dissolved. Return pan to heat. Boil rapidly, stirring continuously and skimming off any scum that rises, until jam reaches setting point (see Lemon Marmalade) or temperature on sugar thermometer reaches 220°F (105°C).

4 Remove from heat. Allow jam to cool for about 10 minutes before filling jars. Allow jam to cool thoroughly before sealing.

MAKES ABOUT 6½ LBS (3 KG)

Chop plums into sections and remove pits

Simmer plums until tender

Remove pan from heat, add sugar and stir until dissolved. Return to heat and boil.

CHERRIES *in* BRANDY

1½ cups (375 mL) sugar

1 cup (250 mL) water

strip of orange or lemon peel

3 lbs (1.5 kg) cherries, pitted

brandy

5 cloves

1 inch (2.5 cm) piece cinnamon

1 Place sugar, water and peel in a saucepan. Bring to a boil, stirring until sugar dissolves. Reduce heat. Simmer for 10 minutes, without stirring.

2 Add cherries. Simmer for a further 5 minutes. Spoon cherries into clean dry jars, reserving syrup. Half fill jars with brandy. Add cloves and cinnamon. Top up jars with reserved syrup.

3 Seal jars. Label. Store in a cool place for 1 month before using. Preserves will keep for up to 12 months.

NOTE: Other stone fruits may be used. Peel, halve and pit before continuing.

MAKES 3 LBS (1.5 KG)

PLUM BUTTER

2 lbs (1 kg) plums

sugar

1 tsp (5 mL) ground cinnamon

1 Barely cover plums with water. Cook, covered, very slowly until tender. Push through sieve, discarding pits.

2 Measure purée. For every cup (250 mL), mix in ⅞ cup (220 mL) sugar. Slowly heat, stirring until sugar dissolves.

3 Add cinnamon. Boil for about ¾ hour until a spoon drawn across pan leaves a clean line behind it. Pour into warm sterilized jars. Seal.

MAKES ABOUT 3 CUPS (750 mL)

APRICOT CHUTNEY

2 lbs (1 kg) apricots, halved and pitted

2 cups (500 mL) brown sugar

2 onions, thinly sliced

¾ cup (185 mL) sultanas

1 tbsp (15 mL) salt

1 tsp (5 mL) coriander seeds

½ tsp (2.5 mL) ground ginger

1 cup (250 mL) white wine vinegar

1 Simmer all ingredients together until apricots are soft – about 15 to 20 minutes. Transfer apricots to warm, sterilized jars.

2 Boil rest of chutney until it is thick and syrupy. Pour over apricots. Seal.

NOTE: Peaches may be substituted for apricots.

MAKES ABOUT 4 CUPS (1 L)

PEACH CHUTNEY

11 lbs (5 kg) peaches, peeled, halved and pitted

5½ cups (1.2 L) sugar

1 cup (250 ml) salt

1 oz (30 g) ground allspice

1 oz (30 g) ground cloves

3 cloves garlic, peeled and chopped

½ oz (15 g) peppercorns, ground

6 cups (1.5 L) white vinegar

1 Boil all ingredients together for 3 hours or until thick. Pour into warm, sterilized jars. Seal.

NOTE: Plums may be substituted for peaches.

MAKES ABOUT 10 CUPS (2.5 L)

FRUITS
from the
VINE

Grapes, passionfruit and kiwis fall into this category. Melons are also grown on vines, but we have devoted a whole chapter to them alone.

Grapes have been cultivated for thousands of years, mainly to produce wine. Today, the grapes we consume with enthusiasm are specifically grown for eating. Perfect with cheese, in desserts or used to enhance certain seafood or chicken dishes and salads, grapes also make lovely garnishes. Handle these delicate fruits with care and look for bunches without any trace of browning.

The kiwi fruit has a fuzzy brown skin which hides its brilliant green, juicy flesh. Perfect as a garnish, kiwi purée is also delicious in mousse, ice cream, sherbet and jam.

The passionfruit vine bears a fragrant fruit with a distinctive sweet-sour flavor. This is one fruit where the crunchy seeds are designed to be eaten! Look for purple fruit with a wrinkled skin. Use them as a garnish or to make jams, drinks or sherbets.

PERFECT CHOICE

Purchase kiwis when firm and allow to ripen at room temperature. Kiwis are ripe when the flesh gives a little between the fingers.

NOTE

Any blue cheese may be substituted for Roquefort.

Turkey and Roquefort Salad with Cranberry Dressing

TURKEY *and* ROQUEFORT SALAD *with* CRANBERRY DRESSING

3 cups (750 mL) diced cooked turkey

1 cup (250 mL) shredded lettuce

1 cup (250 mL) diced celery

½ cup (125 mL) seedless grapes

½ cup (125 mL) toasted pecans, chopped

1½ oz (45 g) Roquefort cheese, crumbled (see note)

CRANBERRY DRESSING

8 oz (225 g) cranberry sauce

¼ cup (60 mL) dark soy sauce

1 small clove garlic, crushed

3 tbsp (45 mL) lemon juice

3 tbsp (45 mL) sherry

1 tbsp (15 mL) vegetable oil

1 Combine turkey, lettuce, celery, grapes and pecans. Pile mixture into shallow serving dish. Crumble Roquefort cheese over top of salad.

2 TO PREPARE CRANBERRY DRESSING: Combine all ingredients in a small saucepan. Heat until well blended. Serve separately in a gravy boat.

SERVES 6

KIWI AND CASHEW SALAD

few lettuce leaves

4 kiwis, peeled and sliced

2 oranges, segmented

6 radishes, thinly sliced

¼ lb (110 g) mushrooms, sliced

1 small cucumber, sliced

2 stalks celery, sliced

¼ cup (60 mL) cashews

vinaigrette dressing to taste

1 Tear lettuce into pieces. Toss all salad ingredients in a salad bowl with nuts and vinaigrette dressing.

SERVES 4

CHICKEN LIVERS VÉRONIQUE

1⅔ lbs (750 g) chicken livers

seasoned flour (see note)

3 tbsp (45 mL) chopped green onions

¼ cup (60 mL) butter or margarine

¼ cup (60 mL) white wine

¼ cup (60 mL) chicken stock

1 tbsp (15 mL) fruit juice

1½ cups (375 mL) seedless grapes

¼ to ½ cup (60 to 125 mL) sour cream

finely chopped parsley to garnish

1 Rinse chicken livers, pat dry. Dust with seasoned flour. Shake off excess.

2 Sauté green onions and livers in butter over medium heat for 6 to 8 minutes. Pour in white wine, stock and fruit juice. Bring to a boil.

3 Add grapes. Reduce heat. Cook, covered, for 3 minutes.

4 Stir in sour cream. Reheat gently. Serve sprinkled with finely chopped parsley.

SERVES 6

BEEF CASSEROLE *with* KIWIS

2 lbs (1 kg) round or topside steak

2 to 3 kiwis, peeled and sliced

1 tbsp (15 mL) oil

1 onion, sliced

1 red pepper, sliced

1 tbsp (15 mL) all-purpose flour

1 cup (250 mL) beef stock

1 tbsp (15 mL) soy sauce

1 tbsp (15 mL) Dijon mustard

freshly ground black pepper to taste

1 Rub meat all over with a few slices of kiwi. Cut meat into 6 pieces. Allow to stand for 10 to 15 minutes.

2 Brown steak pieces in hot oil. Remove meat. Sauté onions and red pepper in same pan until tender.

3 Stir in flour. Cook, stirring, until brown. Stir in stock, soy sauce, mustard and pepper.

4 Return meat to pan with remaining kiwi slices. Simmer, covered, over low heat for 1 hour or until tender.

SERVES 6

Chicken Livers Véronique

 KIWI COOK'S TIP

The flesh of kiwi fruit contains an enzyme that tenderizes meat.

 **HOW TO MAKE SEASONED FLOUR**

Seasoned flour is plain all-purpose flour combined with seasonings of choice, eg. salt, pepper, ground ginger, or dried herbs, to give added flavor.

*Grapes are best skinned
and seeded when used in
cooked dishes. To skin
grapes, dip in boiling
water for a few seconds.
Skin is easily peeled back
with the fingers. Remove
seeds by making a slit in
one side and flicking out
the seeds with the point
of a knife.*

BROILED CORNISH HENS *with* GRAPES

**2 Cornish hens, halved and
backbones removed**

2 tbsp (30 mL) butter or margarine, melted

squeeze of lemon juice

salt and pepper to taste

RED WINE SAUCE

backbones from birds

1 tbsp (15 mL) vegetable oil

1 small onion, chopped

**¼ cup (60 mL) red grapes, seeded
and chopped**

¾ cup (185 mL) chicken stock

½ cup (125 mL) dry fruity red wine

¼ tsp (1 mL) thyme

½ small bay leaf

8 red grapes, halved and seeded

8 seedless green grapes, halved

2 tsp (10 mL) butter

1 tsp (5 mL) Dijon mustard

*Broiled Cornish Hens
with Grapes*

1 Brush Cornish hens with melted butter and lemon juice. Sprinkle with salt and pepper. Set aside.

2 TO PREPARE SAUCE: Brown backbones in oil. Sauté onion and grapes lightly until light brown in color.

3 Add chicken stock, wine, thyme and bay leaf. Bring to a boil. Simmer to reduce to ⅔ cup (165 mL). Strain stock. Cover. Chill.

4 Soften red and green grape halves in butter. Stir in reserved stock. Cook gently till reduced and slightly thickened. Whisk in mustard.

5 TO PREPARE CORNISH HENS: Cook under a hot broiler skin side down for 4 to 5 minutes, brushing frequently with remaining butter and lemon juice.

6 Turn, baste and broil a further 6 minutes. Longer time may be required depending on size of bird. Test with a skewer. Juices will run clear when cooked.

7 Serve the Cornish hens with a little sauce. Serve remaining sauce separately.

SERVES 4

STEP-BY-STEP TECHNIQUES

LEMON SOLE *with* GRAPES

1 whole lemon sole or silver dory, filleted and skinned

2 tbsp (30 mL) butter or margarine

¼ cup (60 mL) green onions, chopped

1 bouquet garni

1 cup (250 mL) fish stock (see note)

salt and white pepper to taste

¼ lb (110 g) green grapes

1 tbsp (15 mL) Calvados or brandy

2 tsp (10 mL) flour

¼ cup (60 mL) dry white wine

¼ cup (60 mL) cream

1 Check fillets for bones. Roll up fillets, starting with tail end. Secure with kitchen string.

2 Melt half of butter in a heavy-based frying pan with a lid. Add green onions, reserving 2 tbsp (30 mL). Fry over low heat until soft.

3 Add bouquet garni, fish stock and fish. Season. Simmer, covered, for 5 to 10 minutes or until the fish flakes when tested.

4 While fish is cooking, soak grapes in Calvados for 15 minutes.

5 When fish is cooked, drain, remove string and keep warm on a serving dish. Strain cooking liquid, reserving ½ cup (125 mL).

6 In a clean pan, melt remaining butter. Sauté remaining green onions until soft. Add flour. Cook, stirring, for 1 minute. Gradually add wine off the heat. Return to heat. Simmer until reduced by a quarter.

7 Add reserved stock. Bring to a boil, then simmer for 5 minutes. Taste and adjust seasoning.

8 Stir in cream and grapes. Heat through gently. Pour over fish.

Lemon Sole with Grapes

Roll up fillets and tie securely with string

Place fillets in fish stock mixture and simmer gently until fish flakes when tested

To make sauce, add wine to cooked green onions and simmer to reduce by a quarter

NOTE: Prepare fish stock by covering fish heads and bones with water. Add some chopped vegetables and a few peppercorns. Simmer for 20 minutes. Strain and use immediately. Do not store.

SERVES 4

Summer Fruit Meringue

SUMMER FRUIT MERINGUE

4 egg whites

1 cup (250 mL) white sugar

1 mango, peeled, seeded and sliced

2 kiwis, peeled and sliced

KIWI FRUIT SAUCE

3 kiwis, peeled and puréed

1 tbsp (15 mL) icing sugar

juice of ½ lemon

MANGO SAUCE

1 mango, peeled, seeded and puréed

1 tbsp (15 mL) icing sugar

juice of ½ lime

1 Whisk egg whites until stiff peaks form. Gradually add sugar, beating until dissolved. Line a baking sheet with aluminum foil. Spoon meringue into the middle and smooth with spatula to make a 9 inch (22 cm) circle.

2 Using fork, fluff the sides to give an uneven texture, leaving a hollow in the middle.

3 Bake at 250°F (120°C) for 1¼ hours. Allow to cool in the oven with the door ajar. Peel away aluminum foil.

4 TO PREPARE KIWI FRUIT SAUCE: Purée kiwis with icing sugar and lemon juice. Pass through sieve to remove black seeds. Chill well.

5 TO PREPARE MANGO SAUCE: Purée mangoes with icing sugar and lime juice. Chill thoroughly.

6 Spoon Mango Sauce on half a 10 inch (25 cm) serving plate (with sides). Spoon the Kiwi Fruit Sauce onto the other half.

7 Place the meringue shell on top of sauce. Fill the hollow with fruit. Place mango slices on the same side as the Kiwi Sauce and the kiwi slices on the Mango Sauce side. Dust with icing sugar to serve.

SERVES 8

KIWI *and* MANGO SHERBET

6 kiwis, peeled and sliced

1 ripe mango, peeled, pitted and sliced

1¼ cups (310 mL) sugar syrup (see note)

1 tbsp (15 mL) orange juice

1 Purée the kiwis and mango in food processor. Add sugar syrup and orange juice. Blend well.

2 Pour mixture into freezer tray. Freeze 1 hour or until ice crystals form.

3 Remove. Process in food processor. Pour mixture back into tray. Refreeze.

4 Just before serving, spoon into chilled dishes with extra slices of the 2 fruits for garnish.

NOTE: To make sugar syrup, dissolve 1 cup (250 mL) sugar in 1 cup (250 mL) water. Bring to a boil. Remove from heat, cool. Store covered in refrigerator until needed.

SERVES 6

PASSIONFRUIT MOUSSE

2 eggs, separated

¼ cup (60 mL) white sugar

rind and juice of 1 lime or lemon

1¼ cups (310 mL) whipping cream, whipped

pulp of 4 passionfruit

1 Whisk egg yolks and sugar in a large bowl until thick and creamy. Add rind and juice. Mix well.

2 Fold in whipped cream and passionfruit. Beat egg whites until soft peaks form. Lightly fold into cream mixture.

3 Spoon into serving dishes. Refrigerate until very cold. Serve with slices of fresh fruit or Passionfruit Sauce (recipe page 63).

SERVES 4–6

COOK'S TIP

Always ensure that whipping cream is cold before whipping or it may curdle.

TO PEEL KIWIS WITH EASE

Kiwi fruit are very easily peeled. Simply use a sharp knife to top and tail the fruit. With the tip of a knife, peel the skin away lengthwise.

Kiwi and Mango Sherbet

Grape and Wine Custard

½ lb (225 g) black grapes

¼ cup (60 mL) brandy

1 egg white

¼ cup (60 mL) sugar

1 Boil white wine and lemon rind 2 minutes. Blend egg yolks with 1/2 the sugar. Mix cornstarch with water to form a smooth paste. Whisk into yolks. Gradually stir in hot wine.

2 Cook yolk mixture in top of double boiler over simmering water until thick, stirring all the time. Remove from heat.

3 Whisk 4 egg whites until stiff peaks form. Add remaining sugar gradually, beating until thick and glossy. Fold in warmed egg custard with lemon juice.

4 Reserve some grapes for decoration. Halve and seed remaining grapes. Soak in brandy.

5 Beat remaining egg white. Dip rims of 6 tall glasses first into beaten egg white, then into sugar. Dip reserved grapes into beaten egg white and sugar. Allow to dry. Chill.

6 Just before serving, divide brandied grapes between glasses. Top up with custard mixture. Decorate with chilled frosted grapes.

SERVES 6

GRAPE *and* WINE CUSTARD

THE FROSTING ON THE GRAPE

Simply dip grapes in lightly beaten egg white followed by white sugar. Let dry on wax paper.

1¼ cups (310 mL) sweet white wine

grated rind of 1 lemon

4 eggs, separated

½ cup (125 mL) white sugar

3 tbsp (45 mL) cornstarch

¼ cup (60 mL) water

juice of ½ lemon

½ lb (225 g) white muscat grapes

FIG *and* PASSIONFRUIT JAM

1 lb (450 g) fresh figs, sliced

1 cup (250 mL) passionfruit pulp

sugar

1 Boil figs and passionfruit together for 10 minutes. Measure and allow 1 cup (250 mL) sugar to each 1 cup (250 mL) fruit.

2 Blend in sugar. Boil again until a little tested on a cold saucer wrinkles when touched.

3 Pour into warm, sterilized jars. Seal when cold.

MAKES ABOUT 3 CUPS (750 mL)

PASSIONFRUIT PUNCH

1 cup (250 mL) sugar

½ cup (125 mL) water

1 cup (250 mL) orange juice

1 cup (250 mL) lemon juice

1 cup (250 mL) passionfruit pulp

ice cubes

1 bottle sparkling white wine

orange and lemon slices to garnish

1 Bring sugar and water to a boil, stirring constantly. Continue to boil for 5 minutes. Allow to cool.

2 Add orange and lemon juices and passionfruit. Chill until needed.

3 To serve, place a good quantity of ice cubes in punch bowl. Pour reserved fruit syrup over ice. Mix in wine. Garnish with orange and lemon slices.

MAKES 6 CUPS (1.5 L)

PASSIONA

1½ cups (375 mL) water

1½ cups (375 mL) sugar

1½ tsp (7.5 mL) cream of tartar

pulp of 48 passionfruit

1 Heat water, sugar and cream of tartar together, stirring, until sugar dissolves. Bring to a boil. Simmer 3 to 4 minutes.

2 While still boiling, add passionfruit, beating with a fork for 3 minutes to extract all the juice. Pour into bowl, and mix well. Bottle and refrigerate.

3 To serve, add a small quantity to a glass of water or soda water. If well corked, it will keep for some time.

MAKES 2½ CUPS (625 mL)

PASSIONFRUIT SAUCE

½ cup (125 mL) white sugar

1 cup (250 mL) water

4 passionfruit

1 Dissolve sugar in water in a small saucepan over a low heat. Bring to a boil. Simmer until liquid has reduced by half. Stir in passionfruit pulp. Simmer for 2 minutes. Cool. Serve with desserts of choice or over ice cream.

MAKES ABOUT 1½ CUPS (375 mL)

BRANDIED GRAPE PRESERVE

1⅓ cups (335 mL) red wine vinegar

1½ cups (375 mL) red wine

¾ cup (185 mL) sugar

3 cloves

4 sticks cinnamon

3 tbsp (45 mL) brandy

2 lbs (1 kg) black grapes, seeded

1 Bring vinegar, wine, sugar, cloves and cinnamon sticks to a boil. Simmer for 15 minutes or until syrupy.

2 Remove cinnamon sticks. Add brandy. Pour over grapes. Put into warm, sterilized jars. Seal.

NOTE: Serve with terrines, game birds and venison.

MAKES ABOUT 4 CUPS (1 L)

TO PREPARE BOUQUET GARNI

A bouquet garni is a flavoring easily prepared by tying together herbs and celery studded with peppercorns. Add to dish during cooking. Alternatively, wrap herbs in cheesecloth, or use the commercially-prepared variety.

MELONS

Nothing beats a slice of icy cold melon on a hot day. Their juicy sweetness
leaves you ready for more. A melon's flesh is just about 95 percent water,
so is it any wonder that they are just as refreshing as a cool drink?

Melons come in lots of shapes and sizes, but the most popular ones
here are watermelons, cantaloupes and honeydew melons
(although others are available).

Eat melons when they are perfectly ripe for optimum flavor.
Aroma is a good way to test this – they usually taste like they smell!

Watermelons are more difficult to test for ripeness due to their thick skin.
Choose those that are firm with even coloration. It is best to purchase
a piece from a cut melon – look for firm, crisp, brightly colored
flesh and a soft waxy rind.

Melons keep well in the refrigerator. If unripe when purchased,
leave at room temperature for a few days until ripe,
and then store in the refrigerator.

Melons are quite versatile and, due to their sweet, juicy flesh, complement
many foods and flavorings. The recipes we have chosen for this section
demonstrate this by teaming them with seafood, pastry and curry,
to name but a few.

Two-Melon Summer Soup

This soup looks beautiful served in glass bowls.

1⅔ lbs (750 g) cantaloupe

3 tbsp (45 mL) fresh lemon juice

2 ripe honeydew melons, 2 lbs (1 kg) each

¼ cup (60 mL) fresh lime juice

2 tsp (10 mL) finely chopped fresh mint

mint sprigs to garnish

cream to garnish, if desired

1 Halve cantaloupe. Scoop out and discard the seeds. Peel and chop. Purée the cantaloupe with the lemon juice in a food processor until smooth. Chill in a covered bowl for at least 12 hours.

2 Halve honeydew. Scoop out and discard the seeds. Peel and chop. Purée the honeydew melon with lime juice and mint in a food processor until smooth. Chill separately in a covered bowl for 12 hours.

3 To serve, place the purées into separate jugs. Pour at the same time, but from separate sides, into chilled serving bowls. The soup should stay in separate colors. Garnish with mint sprigs, and a swirl of cream if desired.

SERVES 6

MELON SHAPES

Melon flesh may be sliced, diced or cut into balls using a melon baller (which come in varying sizes).

Honeydew Melon *with* Crab

2 honeydew melons, halved and seeded

6½ oz (180 g) can crabmeat, drained and flaked

½ cup (125 mL) cream

½ cup (125 mL) mayonnaise

½ to 1 tsp (2.5 to 5 mL) curry powder

mint or parsley to garnish

1 Scoop all flesh from melons with a melon baller. Reserve melon shells.

2 Mix remaining ingredients together. Combine with melon balls.

3 Spoon into melon halves. Garnish with mint or parsley. Chill thoroughly before serving.

SERVES 4

Watermelon Soup

4½ lbs (2 kg) watermelon flesh, seeded

2 cups (500 mL) sweet white wine

¼ cup (60 mL) honey

½ tsp (2.5 mL) garam masala

grated rind and juice of 1 orange

grated rind of 1 lemon

1 cup (250 mL) sour cream

grated nutmeg and dill sprigs to garnish

1 Bring watermelon, wine, honey, garam masala, orange rind and juice and lemon rind to a boil, stirring constantly. Reduce heat. Simmer for 20 minutes. Allow to cool.

2 Purée in blender or food processor. Transfer to a bowl. Stir in sour cream. Chill thoroughly before serving.

3 Serve garnished with dill sprigs and a light sprinkling of grated nutmeg.

SERVES 6

A SERVING SUGGESTION

Melon skins, once hollowed out, make useful serving containers for salads, sherbet, ice cream etc.

THIRST QUENCHERS

Melons make delicious drinks when blended in a blender or food processor.

Two-melon Summer Soup

Melon with prosciutto or seafood is a delicious beginning to any meal.

CANTALOUPE SOUP

1⅔ lbs (750 g) cantaloupe, halved and seeded

½ lb (225 g) seedless grapes

½ lb (225 g) apricots, halved and pitted

1 apple, peeled, cored and sliced

3 cups (750 mL) dry white wine

3 to 4 tbsp (45 to 60 mL) lemon juice

1½ tsp (7.5 mL) cornstarch

1 tbsp (15 mL) honey

¼ cup (60 mL) pine nuts

1 Remove flesh from half the cantaloupe and chop. Scoop flesh from remaining half into balls using a melon baller.

2 Simmer chopped melon, grapes, apricots, apple, wine and lemon juice for 20 minutes. Allow to cool. Purée in a food processor.

3 Return purée to saucepan. Blend cornstarch with a little water to form a smooth paste. Stir cornstarch and honey into soup. Bring to a boil, stirring constantly. Simmer for 3 minutes.

4 Stir in melon balls. Chill thoroughly. Toast pine nuts by tossing in a dry frying pan over low heat until golden. Nuts may also be toasted by spreading in a single layer on a baking sheet and baking at 300°F (150°C) until golden. Sprinkle over soup when serving.

Cantaloupe Soup

SERVES 6

SPICY MELON SALAD

If you really need to prepare the salad in advance, cut the avocado and toss in a little lemon juice to help prevent browning.

½ cantaloupe, balled or sliced

½ honeydew melon, balled or sliced

1 cup (250 mL) diced seeded watermelon

3 green onions, chopped

¼ lb (110 g) prosciutto, cut into strips

1 avocado, sliced

¼ cup (60 mL) sliced sun-dried tomatoes

DRESSING

¼ cup (60 mL) olive oil

3 tbsp (45 mL) white wine vinegar

1 tsp (5 mL) curry powder

few drops chili pepper sauce

seasonings to taste

1 Arrange all ingredients for salad on a shallow serving platter or individual serving plates.

2 TO PREPARE DRESSING: Combine all ingredients in a screw-top jar. Shake well. Pour over salad just before serving. Serve as a starter or a light lunch.

SERVES 6–8

Simmer fruit, lemon juice and wine for 20 minutes

Cool, then purée mixture using a sieve or in a food processor

Add cornstarch mixture and honey to purée and cook until slightly thickened

*Poached Scallops with
Melon, Mango and Snow
Peas in Sesame Dill
Dressing*

POACHED SCALLOPS *with* MELON, MANGO *and* SNOW PEAS *in* SESAME DILL DRESSING

12 uncooked fresh scallops

1 oz (28 g) pickled ginger, chopped

3 tbsp (45 mL) dry white wine

1 small honeydew or cantaloupe, scooped into balls with a melon baller

1 mango, peeled and thinly sliced

¼ lb (110 g) snow peas, blanched and chopped

6 cherry tomatoes, halved

4 asparagus spears, halved lengthwise and cooked

SESAME DILL DRESSING

juice of 1 lemon

2 tsp (10 mL) chopped dill

3 to 4 drops sesame oil

vegetable oil

salt and freshly ground pepper, to taste

1 Combine scallops and ginger and allow to stand for 20 minutes.

2 Heat wine. Blanch scallops and ginger in boiling wine for 1 minute. Drain to remove all pickling solution. Cool.

3 Toss all ingredients except asparagus in Sesame Dill Dressing. Arrange the salad ingredients on 4 chilled plates. Garnish with asparagus spears.

4 TO PREPARE SESAME DILL DRESSING:
Combine lemon juice, dill and sesame oil in a measuring cup. Top with oil to bring up to ⅔ cup (165 mL). Season with salt and pepper. Pour into a screw-top jar. Shake well.

SERVES 4

TO MICROWAVE ASPARAGUS

To cook asparagus: Rinse well. Place in a shallow microwave-safe dish. Cover with plastic wrap. Cook on HIGH (100%) for one minute or until tender.

Step-by-Step Techniques

Add chopped ginger to mixture of coriander seeds, curry powder, onion and flour

Slowly blend in stock, then bring to a boil

Stir in coconut, mixed fruits and cream

Fruit Curry

Fruit Curry

4 to 5 pieces crystallized ginger

2 onions, peeled and chopped

¼ cup (60 mL) butter or margarine

1 tbsp (15 mL) curry powder

1 tbsp (15 mL) all-purpose flour

1 tsp (5 mL) crushed coriander seeds

2 cups (500 mL) chicken stock

2 tsp (10 mL) lemon juice

salt and freshly ground black pepper

3 cups (750 mL) shredded coconut

4 to 5 cups (1 to 1.25 L) chopped mixed fruits (melons, peaches, plums, grapes, bananas, apples, pears)

3 to 4 tbsp (45 to 60 mL) cream

1 Cover ginger with hot water for a few minutes to remove sugar. Drain. Pat dry. Chop finely.

2 Fry onions in butter until tender. Stir in curry powder, flour and coriander seeds and ginger. Cook gently for 5 minutes.

3 Gradually blend in stock. Bring to a boil. Stir in lemon juice and seasonings. Simmer for 30 minutes.

4 Stir in coconut, prepared fruits and cream. Serve hot or cold with rice.

SERVES 4

Fruit Flan

Pastry Base

4 sheets ready-made shortcrust pastry

1 egg, beaten

Filling

1 lb (450 g) cream cheese, softened

1 cup (250 mL) white sugar

1 tsp (5 mL) cinnamon

juice and grated rind of 1 lemon

Topping

1 honeydew melon, seeded and
scooped into balls

²⁄₃ lb (300 g) black grapes, stems removed

½ cantaloupe, seeded and
scooped into balls

3 feijoas or kiwis, sliced

pulp of 2 passionfruit

1 strawberry

Glaze

1 cup (250 mL) apricot jam, warmed
and strained

½ cup (125 mL) orange juice or water

1 Preheat oven to 400°F (200°C). Join 2
pastry sheets together, pressing joint firmly.
Repeat with remaining 2 sheets.

2 Lightly grease 2 x 9 inch (22 cm) flan or
quiche pans. Press pastry gently into base.
Bake blind (see note) for 10 minutes.

3 Remove baking beans. Prick pastry base
with fork. Cool completely before filling.
Do not fill more than 3 hours before serving.

4 To Prepare Filling: Combine filling
ingredients until smooth and creamy. Spoon
equal amounts into the flan shells. Smooth
top of each with a spatula. Refrigerate until
firm (about 1 hour).

5 Top decoratively with prepared fruit.

6 To Prepare Glaze: Combine
ingredients. Lightly brush over fruit. Chill
before serving.

Fruit Flan

 To Bake Blind

*Cover pastry with a piece
of kitchen parchment
or foil.*

*Cover with dried beans,
peas, rice or pasta. Bake
according to instructions.
Remove paper and beans.
Continue as directed.*

Fresh *from the* Tropics

Many fruits can be classified as tropical, and in this section we have included fruits such as pineapples, bananas, mangoes, papayas, lychees and other exotic, less well-known fruit, grown in hot climates. These fruits are mostly soft-fleshed and are delicious in mousses, ice cream, sherbets and jelly.

Mangoes are a favorite of many – with good reason, as they are one of the most delicious tropical fruits. They are still fairly expensive, but one taste of that sweet, juicy flesh makes the cost worthwhile. Select those with shiny, unblemished skins that if squeezed gently will give slightly.

They will ripen in a warm room, and keep well if refrigerated.

Pineapples are another very popular tropical fruit which grow straight out of the ground. They are sweet, aromatic and acidic all at once, which makes them delicious in salads or even as an accompaniment to pork or ham.

The oriental fruit lychee and its relative the rambutan are best served whole to really appreciate their flavor. In this chapter, we have some lovely serving suggestions for these fruits.

TANGY MANGO *and* CUCUMBER SOUP

3 green onions, chopped

1 mango, peeled, seeded and puréed

½ cup (125 mL) lemon juice

½ cup (125 mL) orange and mango juice

½ cup (125 mL) plain low-fat yogurt

1 clove garlic, crushed

1½ cucumbers, peeled, seeded and grated

salt and freshly ground pepper, to taste

½ red pepper, finely diced

1 Place green onions, mango, lemon juice, orange and mango juice, yogurt and garlic in a food processor or blender. Process until smooth. Transfer to a serving bowl. Add grated cucumber and seasonings.

2 Chill until ready to serve. Garnish with sliced cucumber and finely diced red pepper.

SERVES 4

CUSTARD APPLE SOUP

2 medium-size ripe custard apples or papayas

2 cups (500 mL) chicken stock

juice of 2 limes

1 cup (250 mL) sour cream

salt and freshly ground pepper, to taste

lemon slices and dill sprigs to garnish

1 Scoop out flesh of custard apples, discarding seeds. Purée in blender or food processor, gradually adding stock, until smooth. Blend in lime juice.

2 Transfer mixture to bowl. Stir in sour cream and seasonings. Serve in bowls garnished with lemon slices and dill.

SERVES 4

MILD CURRY *and* MANGO SOUP

1 mango, peeled and flesh removed or 16 oz (450 g) can mango slices

2 cups (500 mL) chicken stock

juice of ½ lemon

¼ tsp (1 mL) curry powder

salt and freshly ground pepper, to taste

½ cup (125 mL) cream

1 tsp (5 mL) saffron threads

1 Place mango, stock and lemon juice in a food processor or blender. Process until smooth.

2 Add curry powder and seasonings. Gently heat soup until hot. Do not allow to boil. Stir in cream before serving.

3 If serving cold, there is no need to cook the soup, just purée with the seasonings and cream.

4 Serve with croutons or crusty bread and garnish with a few saffron threads.

SERVES 4

LYCHEE COCKTAIL

½ lb (225 g) lychees or rambutans, peeled, halved and seeded

1 cup (250 mL) diced pineapple

1 cup (250 mL) diced orange

1 tbsp (15 mL) sugar

2 tsp (10 mL) lemon juice

1 Combine fruits. Chill for 1 hour. Stir in sugar and lemon juice. Serve in chilled cocktail glasses.

SERVES 4

Pizza Supreme

1 tsp (5 mL) white sugar

⅓ cup (85 mL) warm water

1 tsp (5 mL) dry yeast

½ cup (125 mL) whole-wheat flour

½ cup (125 mL) all-purpose flour

2 tsp (10 mL) butter

2 tsp (10 mL) oil

TOPPING

4 tbsp (60 mL) tomato paste

1 tomato, sliced

1 onion, sliced

2 oz (60 g) mushrooms, sliced

2 oz (60 g) salami, sliced

3 slices pineapple, chopped

12 black olives

6 anchovy fillets

½ lb (225 g) mozzarella cheese, sliced

1 Dissolve sugar in water. Stir in yeast. Set aside in warm place until frothy.

2 Mix together flours. Cut in butter. Add yeast, liquid and oil. Mix until sides of bowl are clean.

3 Knead dough on lightly floured surface. Clean bowl. Lightly oil it and leave dough in it, covered, to rise until double in size.

4 Punch down dough. Knead until smooth. Pat dough into a 9-inch (22 cm) pizza pan. Brush with oil. Let stand for 15 minutes before baking.

5 TO PREPARE TOPPING: Spread pizza base with tomato paste. Arrange other topping ingredients over paste. Bake at 400°F (200°C) for 25 to 30 minutes.

MAKES 1 PIZZA

PERFECT PINEAPPLE PIECES

After peeling pineapples, make sure all of the hard, unpalatable 'eyes' are removed before serving.

Pizza Supreme

*Racks of Lamb with
Parsley Mint Crust*

RACKS *of* LAMB *with* PARSLEY MINT CRUST

¼ cup (60 mL) butter or margarine

1 tbsp (15 mL) mango chutney

2 tsp (10 mL) Dijon mustard

1 clove garlic, crushed

2 tsp (10 mL) lemon juice

6 racks of lamb (3 chops each),
excess fat trimmed

½ cup (125 mL) finely chopped fresh parsley

3 tbsp (45 mL) finely chopped fresh mint

salt and freshly ground black pepper

MANGO MINT SAUCE

1 mango, peeled, seeded and puréed

1 tbsp (15 mL) finely chopped fresh mint

freshly ground black pepper

1 tsp (5 mL) vinegar

1 Combine butter, chutney, mustard, garlic and lemon juice. Spread evenly over the back of each lamb rack.

2 Sprinkle with parsley, mint and seasonings. Press onto lamb using the back of a metal spoon.

3 Bake at 400°F (200°C) for 20 to 30 minutes or until tender.

4 TO PREPARE SAUCE: Combine ingredients in a small saucepan. Heat gently, then serve.

SERVES 6

PORK SALAD *with* GINGER MANGO DRESSING

1 head lettuce, washed and drained

**1⅓ lbs (600 g) pork fillet, fried and
sliced into medallions**

½ pineapple, peeled and chopped

4 stalks celery, sliced

¼ lb (110 g) hazelnuts, toasted

¼ lb (110 g) mushrooms

**1 mango, peeled, seeded and chopped or
16 oz (450 g) can mango slices**

**1 red apple, sliced and sprinkled
with lemon juice to prevent browning**

salt and freshly ground pepper, to taste

snipped chives

GINGER MANGO DRESSING

2 mangoes, peeled and seeded

⅔ cup (165 mL) mayonnaise

1 tsp (5 mL) ginger

1 Tear lettuce leaves into bite-size pieces,
reserving a few large leaves to line salad
bowl. Mix together remaining ingredients,
except chives. Spoon into serving bowl.

**2 TO PREPARE GINGER MANGO
DRESSING:** Purée mango, mayonnaise and
ginger until smooth.

3 Toss through dressing. Garnish with
chives. Serve.

SERVES 4–6

PEELING LYCHEES AND RAMBUTANS

*When using fresh lychees,
peel by breaking open the
skin and pressing. The
fruit will pop out.
Rambutans only require
peeling with a knife.*

*Pork Salad with Ginger
Mango Dressing*

*Stir-fried Mango
Chicken with Almonds*

STIR-FRIED MANGO CHICKEN *with* ALMONDS

3 chicken breasts, skinned, boned and cut into thin strips

1½ tbsp (20 mL) cornstarch mixed with 1½ tbsp (20 mL) light soy sauce and 3 tbsp (45 mL) sherry

½ cup (125 mL) vegetable oil

1½ tsp (7.5 mL) chopped fresh ginger

1 clove garlic, crushed

4 green onions, white part chopped and green part cut into 1 inch (2.5 cm) pieces

salt and freshly ground pepper

2 mangoes, peeled and cut in long strips

3 tbsp (45 mL) sherry

1 tbsp (15 mL) light soy sauce

1 tsp (5 mL) brown sugar

1 tsp (5 mL) cornstarch

½ cup (125 mL) slivered almonds, toasted

1 Place chicken in a bowl. Spoon cornstarch mixture over chicken strips. Marinate in the refrigerator for 30 minutes. Drain.
2 Heat ¼ cup (60 mL) oil in a wok over high heat. Stir-fry chicken for 30 seconds. Remove. Drain on paper towels.
3 Heat 3 tbsp (45 mL) oil and stir-fry ginger, garlic, white part of the green onions and seasonings for 30 seconds.
4 Reheat chicken in the wok for 1 minute. Place chicken in a serving dish.
5 Heat 1 tbsp (15 mL) of oil in the wok. Add mangoes. Stir-fry for 30 seconds. Stir in sherry, soy sauce, sugar and cornstarch. Cook 30 seconds or until the sauce thickens.
6 Add the green parts of green onions and almonds. Pour over chicken. Garnish with sliced green onions.

SERVES 4

VEAL *with* POMEGRANATES

1 tsp (5 mL) salt

freshly ground black pepper

1 tsp (5 mL) paprika

¼ tsp (1 mL) ground allspice

¼ cup (60 mL) all-purpose flour

2 lbs (1 kg) stewing veal, cut in
1 inch (2.5 cm) cubes

¼ cup (60 mL) oil

1 large onion, peeled and chopped

1 cup (250 mL) veal or chicken stock

1 tbsp (15 mL) tomato paste

juice of 3 large pomegranates

1 tbsp (15 mL) honey

½ cup (125 mL) chopped celery

½ red pepper, seeded, thinly sliced

pomegranate seeds and parsley to garnish

1 Mix salt, pepper, paprika and allspice
with flour. Dust diced veal with seasoned
flour. Shake off excess.
2 Brown veal in oil. Transfer to casserole.
Sauté onion in same pan. Add stock, tomato
paste, pomegranate juice and honey. Mix
well.
3 Pour sauce over veal. Bake, covered, at
300°F (150°C) for 1 hour 45 minutes.
Add celery and red pepper. Bake a further
15 minutes or until meat is tender. Garnish
with pomegranate seeds and parsley.

NOTE: To make pomegranate juice, cut ripe
pomegranates in half and squeeze on lemon
juicer to crush seeds.

SERVES 6

FISH *and* FRUIT SALAD

1 lb (450 g) white fish fillets

¼ cup (60 mL) lemon juice

6 guavas, pitted and diced

3 slices fresh pineapple, diced

3 bananas, sliced

1 large firm ripe mango, peeled,
pitted and diced

1 Spanish onion, thinly sliced

1 red chili pepper, seeded
and finely chopped

¾ cup (185 mL) canned coconut milk

red pepper or snipped chives to garnish

1 Cut fish into narrow strips. Marinate in
lemon juice for at least 6 hours. Drain.
2 Arrange the fish and prepared fruit in a
salad bowl. Garnish with the onion and
chili pepper. Pour on coconut milk. Chill
thoroughly.
3 Garnish with strips of red pepper or
chives. Coconut milk may be served
separately if preferred.

SERVES 4

STORING BANANAS

*Always store bananas at
room temperature. Never
refrigerate or freeze them
as they will turn black.*

Veal with Pomegranates

Coat diced veal with seasoned flour

Brown veal in oil

Pour pomegranate sauce over veal

4 Whip cream. Fold into mixture. Pour into a greased 9 inch (22 cm) ring mold. Let set in refrigerator 3 to 4 hours.

5 Turn pudding onto serving dish. Scoop out flesh from papaya with melon baller. Pile in center of pudding. Garnish with lime slices.

NOTE: When grating rind from lemon or orange, do so gently as only the color is wanted. The white pith is bitter.

SERVES 6

SMOKED TURKEY *with* PAPAYA

Prosciutto can be used instead of turkey for a different flavor.

1 medium-size papaya

12 thin slices smoked turkey breast

lime wedges and watercress sprigs, to garnish

CRANBERRY MAYONNAISE

½ cup (125 mL) mayonnaise

4 tbsp (60 mL) cranberry sauce

1 Peel, halve and remove seeds from papaya. Cut each half lengthwise into thirds.

2 Arrange 2 thin slices of turkey on each portion of papaya. Serve on individual plates, garnished with lime wedges, watercress sprigs and Cranberry Mayonnaise.

3 TO PREPARE CRANBERRY MAYONNAISE: Blend ingredients together well.

SERVES 6

Smoked Turkey with Papaya

SUN GLORY PAPAYA PUDDING

If papaya is not available, substitute any melon.

1¼ cups (310 mL) milk

⅓ cup (85 mL) semolina

3 tbsp (45 mL) gelatine

3 tbsp (45 mL) honey

juice and grated rind of 1 lemon

juice and grated rind of 1 orange

1 cup (250 mL) papaya pulp

⅔ cup (165 mL) whipping cream

1 papaya

2 limes or lemons, thinly sliced

 **EASY PAPAYA**

Papaya is delicious soaked in lime or orange juice.

1 Bring milk to a boil. Stir in semolina. Cook 5 minutes.

2 Blend gelatine and honey. Stir into hot semolina mixture until dissolved.

3 Flavor with lemon and orange rind and juice. Stir in papaya. Cool.

MANGO *and* SHRIMP SALAD

12 shrimp, shelled and deveined

2 mangoes, peeled

¼ lb (110 g) snow peas

4 green onions, chopped

1 cup (250 mL) pecans

salt and freshly ground pepper

3 tbsp (45 mL) vinaigrette or French dressing

Make a small cut to expose vein on tail   *Pull out vein*

1 Halve shrimp if large. Cut large slice from each side of the mango pit, then cut off the remaining flesh. Cut the large mango slices into strips.

2 Blanch snow peas in boiling water for 1 minute. Drain. Cool under cold running water. If preferred, snow peas can be served raw in the salad.

3 Combine shrimp, mango, snow peas, green onions, pecans and seasonings. Pour dressing over. Toss well before serving.

SERVES 4–6

Mango and Shrimp Salad

GINGER MANGO CHEESECAKE

CRUST

2½ cups (625 mL) chocolate wafer crumbs

¼ lb (110 g) butter or margarine, melted

FILLING

¼ cup (60 mL) water

¼ cup (60 mL) lemon juice

1 oz (28 g) package lemon jelly powder

12 oz (375 mL) can evaporated milk, chilled

8 oz (225 mL) soft cream cheese

2 mangoes, peeled, seeded and roughly chopped or 2 x 16 oz (450 g) cans mango slices

¼ cup (60 mL) brown sugar

1 tsp (5 mL) vanilla extract

1 tbsp (15 mL) glacé ginger, finely chopped

1 mango, sliced

whipped cream

1/2 lemon, thinly sliced and cut into small pieces

chocolate curls

1 TO PREPARE CRUST: Combine cookie crumbs and melted butter thoroughly. Press into the bottom and sides of a greased 9 inch (22 cm) springform pan. Chill.

2 TO PREPARE FILLING: Heat water and lemon juice until boiling. Add jelly powder. Stir to dissolve. Allow to cool.

3 Whip evaporated milk until thick. Add cream cheese and mangoes. Beat until smooth. Blend in sugar, vanilla, ginger and jelly mixture. Pour over crumb crust. Chill.

4 Decorate with mango slices, cream, lemon slices and chocolate curls.

SERVES 10–12

Mango Ice Cream

MANGO ICE CREAM

1 mango, peeled, seeded and roughly chopped (see note)

1 papaya, peeled, seeded and roughly chopped

1 tbsp (15 mL) lemon juice

4 egg yolks

⅔ cup (165 mL) icing sugar

¾ cup (185 mL) whipping cream, whipped

1 Purée mango and papaya together with lemon juice in food processor. Set aside.

2 Combine egg yolks and icing sugar in the top of a double boiler. Whisk mixture until eggs are lemon-color and thick. Remove from heat. Whisk a further 2 minutes.

3 Fold the fruit purée gently into the egg mixture. Blend in cream.

4 Pour into decorative 4-cup (1 L) metal mold. Freeze for a minimum of 3 hours.

5 To remove, dip the mold in warm water for 30 seconds. Turn out onto a serving platter or scoop out as ice cream balls.

NOTE: Canned mangoes can also be used in this recipe.

SERVES 6–8

TROPICAL SHERBET

MANGO SHERBET

2 mangoes, peeled, seeded and puréed

1¼ cups (310 mL) water

⅔ cup (165 mL) white sugar

KIWI FRUIT SHERBET

4 kiwis, peeled and puréed

1¾ cups (440 mL) water

1 cup (250 mL) white sugar

juice and grated rind of 1 lemon

PINEAPPLE SHERBET

1¾ cups (440 mL) pineapple juice

⅔ cup (165 mL) water

⅔ cup (165 mL) white sugar

2 to 3 drops orange extract

fresh mint, to garnish

1 Spoon the 2 fruit purées and the pineapple juice into 3 separate bowls. Set aside.

2 TO PREPARE SUGAR SYRUPS: Place water and the required amount of sugar into 3 separate saucepans. Stir until sugar dissolves.

3 Boil syrups for Mango and Kiwi Fruit Sherbets for 5 minutes. Boil syrup for Pineapple Sherbet for 3 minutes. Cool syrups. Add to their respective purées, and blend.

4 Add lemon juice and rind to Kiwi Fruit Sherbet and orange extract to Pineapple Sherbet.

5 Pour each mixture into separate freezer trays. Freeze for 2½ hours. Remove from freezer. Process in blender to break up the ice crystals. Return to freezer until frozen.

6 Allow sherbets to soften for 10 minutes at room temperature before serving. Place scoops of sherbet on chilled trays. Return to the freezer for 30 minutes to harden.

7 Arrange the sherbet scoops colorfully on individual serving plates. Garnish with mint.

SERVES 4–6

Tropical Sherbet

TROPICAL FRUIT CAKE

3 cups (750 mL) water

1½ cups (375 mL) sugar

4 small mangoes, peeled, seeded and diced

1⅓ lbs (600 g) pineapple, peeled, cored and diced

1⅓ lbs (600 g) cherries, stems and pits removed

4 cups (1 L) all-purpose flour

2 tsp (10 mL) dry yeast

1 cup (250 mL) warm milk

¼ lb (110 g) butter or margarine, cut into small pieces

Tropical Fruit Cake

5 tbsp (75 mL) sugar

¼ cup (60 mL) ground hazelnuts

1 tsp (5 mL) vanilla extract

salt to taste

TOPPING

2 cups (500 mL) all-purpose flour

1¼ cups (310 mL) brown sugar

1½ tsp (7.5 mL) cinnamon

⅓ lb (150 g) butter or margarine, melted

1 Combine water and sugar in a saucepan. Stir until sugar is dissolved. Bring to a boil. Boil, without stirring, for 10 minutes.

2 Remove pan from the heat. Add mangoes, pineapple and cherries to liquid for 5 minutes each. Remove.

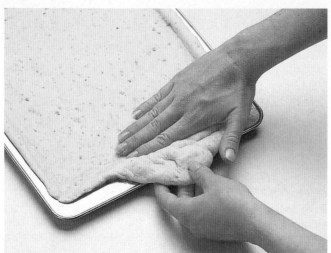

Line pan with dough, forming a lip

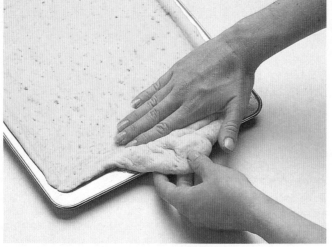

Place cherries in a diagonal row

Arrange other fruits decoratively

A delicious alternative to a traditional Christmas Cake

3 Sift flour into bowl. Make a well in the center. Dissolve the yeast in milk with 1 tsp (5 mL) sugar. Pour into the well. Mix together to form a dough. At this stage the dough will look very dry.

4 Lightly oil a clean bowl. Place dough in bowl. Let rise in a warm place until doubled in size.

5 When the dough has risen sufficiently, add butter, sugar, hazelnuts and vanilla. Work together until dough is smooth and elastic. Place in a lightly greased bowl. Leave to rise in a warm place for about 30 minutes. Knead the dough for 5 minutes. Roll out so it is big enough to fit a greased 8 x 14 inch (22 x 35 cm) pan. Turn the sides down to form a lip. Cover the dough with the fruits in 3 sections.

6 TO PREPARE TOPPING: Combine the flour, sugar, cinnamon and butter in a bowl. Rub together with fingers to form crumbs.

7 Sprinkle the crumble mixture evenly over fruit. Bake at 400°F (200°C) for 35 to 40 minutes.

MAKES 24 PIECES

BANANA SOUFFLÉ

¼ cup (60 mL) butter or margarine
¼ cup (60 mL) all-purpose flour
½ tsp (2.5 mL) vanilla extract
1/2 cup (125 mL) cream
2 ripe medium bananas
¼ cup (60 mL) white sugar
4 eggs, separated
1 tbsp (15 mL) shredded coconut

1 Lightly grease 4 individual 1-cup (250 mL) soufflé dishes. (If desired, fit dishes with paper collars first.) Dust with white sugar.

2 Melt butter in a small saucepan. Stir in flour. Cook 1 minute. Remove from heat. Add vanilla and cream. Beat until smooth. Return to heat. Cook, stirring constantly, until sauce boils and thickens. Place sauce in a bowl. Allow to cool.

3 Mash bananas. Beat bananas, white sugar, and egg yolks into cooled mixture. Combine well.

4 Beat egg whites until stiff peaks form. Gently fold egg whites through banana mixture. Spoon mixture into prepared dishes. Sprinkle each with a little coconut.

5 Bake at 375°F (190°C) for 15 to 20 minutes. Serve immediately with whipped cream.

SERVES 4

BANANA APRICOT BREAD

1 cup (250 mL) chopped dried apricots
¼ cup (60 mL) sherry
1¼ cups (310 mL) all-purpose flour
2 tsp (10 mL) baking powder
½ tsp (2.5 mL) baking soda
6 tbsp (90 mL) butter or margarine
grated rind of 1 lemon
⅔ cup (165 mL) white sugar
2 eggs
½ cup (125 mL) mashed banana

1 Soak apricots in sherry for 1 hour. Drain and discard sherry. Sift flour, baking powder and baking soda twice. Set aside.

2 Cream butter, lemon rind and sugar together. Beat in eggs one at a time. Beat well after each addition. Fold in fruits alternately with flour mixture.

3 Place mixture into a greased and lined 4 x 8 inch (10 x 20 cm) loaf pan. Bake at 350°F (180°C) for 1 hour or until cooked.

4 Cool on wire rack. Ice if desired, with icing of your choice.

MAKES 1 LOAF

PEELING BANANAS

Once peeled or cut, bananas should be tossed in lemon juice to prevent them from going brown.

COOKING BANANAS

Bananas may be cooked in their skin either boiled, baked or broiled.

STEP-BY-STEP TECHNIQUES

PINEAPPLE SHERBET

1 medium pineapple

2 limes

1 ⅔ cups (415 mL) water

¾ cup (185 mL) sugar

mint sprigs for garnish

1 Cut pineapple in half lengthwise, leaving leaves intact. Using grapefruit knife, remove the flesh, leaving shells whole for serving. Place pineapple shells in refrigerator until needed.

2 Peel limes, removing white pith. Cut in quarters. Purée lime and pineapple fruits in food processor.

3 Heat water and sugar, stirring until sugar dissolves. Simmer for 8 to 10 minutes until a thin syrup forms. Allow to cool. Add to pineapple mixture.

4 Pour into freezer trays. Freeze until set. Process again in food processor to break up ice crystals. Pour back into freezer trays. Cover with foil. Allow to refreeze.

5 When ready to serve, dip bottom of trays in hot water. Tip out sherbet. Cut into large dice. Pile sherbet into pineapple shells. Serve garnished with mint sprigs.

SERVES 6

Pineapple Sherbet

Remove flesh using a grapefruit knife

Peel limes and cut into quarters

Pour syrup into puréed fruit

HOT MANGO *and* TOMATO CHUTNEY

6 under-ripe tomatoes, sliced

**4 medium-firm under-ripe mangoes,
peeled, seeded and diced**

2 onions, peeled and chopped

2 cloves garlic, minced

½ inch (1 cm) piece fresh ginger, finely grated

1 cup (250 mL) currants

4 red chili peppers, seeded and sliced

3 tbsp (45 mL) chopped fresh coriander

¼ tsp (1 mL) cayenne pepper

2 cups (500 mL) malt vinegar

2 cups (500 mL) brown sugar

1 tsp (5 mL) salt, optional

1 Place all ingredients in a heavy-based saucepan. Mix well. Bring to a boil, then simmer gently for 10 minutes.

2 Reduce heat to low. Cook, stirring, until mangoes are soft and mixture is a jam-like consistency.

3 Remove from heat. Cool slightly. Bottle chutney in sterilized jars. Remove any air bubbles by piercing mixture with a skewer.

4 Cut out circles of wax paper according to jar size. Place these on top of the chutney. Press lightly with fingertips to remove air.

5 Seal with sterilized lids. Store in a cool place. Refrigerate after opening.

MAKES ABOUT 6 CUPS (1.5 L)

SPICY MANGO SAUCE

2 mangoes, peeled, seeded and puréed

1 tbsp (15 mL) Madeira wine

¼ cup (60 mL) butter or margarine

2 green chili peppers, finely chopped

1 tsp (5 mL) caraway seeds

salt and freshly ground pepper, to taste

1 Combine mango and Madeira until smooth. Melt butter in a small frying pan. Add all ingredients. Simmer, covered, for 8 minutes, stirring occasionally.

2 If sauce becomes too thick, thin with a little water. Store covered in refrigerator. Serve hot or cold with beef, pork, fish, chicken and rice dishes.

MAKES ABOUT 1½ CUPS (375 mL)

Hot Mango and Tomato Chutney

Persimmon Jam

Cut cross in pointed end of persimmon and peel back skin

Cook persimmon pulp and sugar over low heat

Stir in lemon juice, rind and pineapple

PERSIMMON JAM

4 ripe persimmons

2 cups (500 mL) sugar

½ cup (125 mL) grated pineapple

1 tbsp (15 mL) lemon juice

shredded peel of 1 lemon

1 Cut a cross in pointed ends of persimmons. Peel off skin. Discard skin and stem end.

2 Combine persimmon pulp with sugar. Cook over low heat 15 minutes, stirring constantly until thickened and clear. Do not boil.

3 Stir in pineapple, lemon juice and rind. Pour into warm sterilized jars. Seal when cool.

MAKES ABOUT 1½ CUPS (375 ML)

MANGO MINT COOLER

1 mango, peeled, seeded and puréed

½ cup (125 mL) combined orange and mango juice

½ cup (125 mL) lemonade

¼ cup (60 mL) Advocaat

3 tbsp (45 mL) Crème de Menthe

mint leaves, to garnish

1 Combine all ingredients. Blend until smooth. Pour into tall glasses over ice. Garnish with mint leaves.

SERVES 2

TAMARILLO CHUTNEY

1 lb (450 g) brown sugar

½ lb (225 g) apples, peeled, cored and thinly sliced

½ lb (225 g) onions, peeled and finely chopped

12 tamarillos, blanched and diced

1¼ cups (310 mL) white vinegar

2 tsp (10 mL) pickling spice

2 tsp (10 mL) salt

pinch cayenne pepper

1 Place all ingredients in a saucepan and bring to a boil. Reduce heat. Simmer for 45 minutes or until thick, stirring occasionally.

2 Pour into warm, sterilized jars. Seal.

MAKES ABOUT 4 CUPS (1 L)

TAMARILLOS

When ripe, tamarillos should be firm but not hard. They can be cut in half and eaten with a spoon, but if you are cooking them, the skin must be removed as it is bitter. Pour boiling water over them, and leave for 2 minutes, after which the skin will peel off, just like a tomato.

FEIJOA AND GUAVA JELLY

2¾ lbs (1.25 kg) feijoas

2 lbs (1 kg) apples, cored

1 lb (450 g) guavas

sugar

1 Cut up all fruit roughly. Cover with water. Boil for 1 hour or until mushy.

2 Push through a sieve, or strain through a jelly bag or cheesecloth overnight.

3 Measure juice. Allow 3/4 cup (185 mL) sugar to each 1 cup (250 mL) of juice. Bring juice to a boil and add sugar, stirring until dissolved.

4 Boil rapidly for 10 minutes or until a few drops tested on a cold saucer wrinkle when touched.

5 Pour into warm, sterilized jars. Seal when cold.

MAKES ABOUT 6 CUPS (1.5 L)

Feijoa and Guava Jelly

Cut up fruit roughly

Press cooked fruit through sieve

Bring juice to a boil and add sugar

PICK OF THE CROP

PRODUCE	SOUTHERN HEMISPHERE	NORTHERN HEMISPHERE
Apples (Delicious)	All year	All year
Apples (Red)	March to December	October to March
Apples (Green) (Granny Smith)	All year	All year
Apricots	November to February	June to August
Avocados (Alligator Pears)	All year	All year
Bananas	All year	All year
Cantaloupe	All year	July to September
Cherries	October to mid January	May to July
Custard Apple	April to August	June to December
Carambola (Star Fruit)	October to July	June to July
Coconuts	All year	All year
Dates	All year	All year

PRODUCE	SOUTHERN HEMISPHERE	NORTHERN HEMISPHERE
Feijoas	May to August	All year
Figs, Fresh	December to May	July to September
Grapefruit	All year	All year
Grapes (Early Varieties)	November	All year
Grapes (Black Muscat)	December to April	July to May
Grapes (White/Black Varieties)	January to June	All year
Grapes (Sultanas)	January to May	June to July / January to February
Guava	November to May	All year
Honeydew	All year	February to December
Kiwi fruit (Chinese Gooseberry)	All year	All year
Lemons	All year	All year
Limes	June to September	All year
Lychees (Litchis)	November to March	December to March

PRODUCE	SOUTHERN HEMISPHERE	NORTHERN HEMISPHERE
Mandarins (Clementines, Tangerines, Satsuma)	April to October	July to February
Mangoes	November to March	All year
Oranges (Navels)	May to October	November to March / May to July
Oranges (Valencia)	September to April	April to November
Papaya	All year	All year
Passionfruit (Purple Granadilla)	All year	All year
Peaches	November to March	May to September / December to January
Pears	All year	All year
Persimmons (Kaki Fruit, Sharon Fruit, Apple of the Orient)	February to June	October to December
Pineapples	All year	All year
Plums (Early Varieties)	December	July to April
Plums (Wilson)	November to December	July to April
Plums (Blood & others)	December to February	July to April

PRODUCE	SOUTHERN HEMISPHERE	NORTHERN HEMISPHERE
Plums (President)	March to May	July to April
Quinces (Japonicas)	January to May	Mid July
Rhubarb	All year	January to September
Strawberries	All year	June to July
Strawberries (Imported)	May to July	All year
Rambutans	September to May	All year
Tamarillo	March to December	August to September
Watermelon	All year	May to September
Boysenberries	December to February	July to August
Redcurrants, Blackcurrants	December	June to September
Mulberries	October to December	June to September
Blackberries	January to March	August to September
Gooseberries	October to February	June to July
Raspberries	November to February	July to August

MEASURING MADE EASY

HOW TO MEASURE LIQUIDS

CUPS	U.S.	METRIC
2 tablespoons	1 fluid ounce	30 mL
¼ cup	2 fluid ounces	60 mL
	3 fluid ounces	90 mL
½ cup	4 fluid ounces	125 mL
	5 fluid ounces	150 mL
	5 1/2 fluid ounces	170 mL
¾ cup	6 fluid ounces	185 mL
	7 fluid ounces	220 mL
1 cup	8 fluid ounces	250 mL
2 cups	16 fluid ounces (1 pint)	500 mL
2½ cups	20 fluid ounces	625 mL
4 cups	32 fluid ounces (1 quart)	1 liter

HOW TO MEASURE DRY INGREDIENTS

½ oz		15 g
1 oz		30 g
2 oz		60 g
3 oz		90 g
4 oz	(¼ lb)	125 g
5 oz		155 g
6 oz		185 g
7 oz		220 g
8 oz	(½ lb)	250 g
9 oz		280 g
10 oz		315 g
11 oz		345 g
12 oz	(¾ lb)	375 g
13 oz		410 g
14 oz		440 g
15 oz		470 g
16 oz	(1 lb)	500 g
24 oz	(1½ lb)	750 g
32 oz	(2 lb)	1 kg

QUICK CONVERSIONS

¼ inch		5 mm
½ inch		1 cm
¾ inch		2 cm
1 inch		2.5 cm
2 inches		5 cm
2½ inches		6 cm
3¼ inches		8 cm
4 inches		10 cm
5 inches		12 cm
6 inches		15 cm
7 inches		18 cm
8 inches		20 cm
9 inches		22 cm
10 inches		25 cm
11 inches		28 cm
12 inches	(1 foot)	30 cm
18 inches		46 cm
20 inches		50 cm
24 inches	(2 feet)	61 cm
30 inches		77 cm

USING CUPS AND SPOONS

All cup and spoon measurements are level

¼ cup	2 fluid ounces	60 mL	¼ teaspoon		1.25 mL
⅓ cup	2½ fluid ounces	85 mL	½ teaspoon		2.5 mL
½ cup	4 fluid ounces	125 mL	1 teaspoon		5 mL
1 cup	8 fluid ounces	250 mL	1 tablespoon		15 mL

OVEN TEMPERATURES

FAHRENHEIT (°F)	CELSIUS (°C)	TEMPERATURES
250	120	Very slow
300	150	Slow
325-350	160-180	Moderately slow
375-400	190-200	Moderate
425-450	220-230	Moderately hot
475-500	250-260	Hot

INDEX